ADOLESCENT PREGNANCY PREVENTION

ADOLESCENT PREGNANCY PREVENTION —
School-Community Cooperation

By

CONSTANCE HOENK SHAPIRO, Ph.D.

Department of Human Service Studies
New York State College of Human Ecology
Cornell University
Ithaca, New York

CHARLES C THOMAS • PUBLISHER
Springfield • Illinois • U.S.A.

Published and Distributed Throughout the World by

CHARLES C THOMAS • PUBLISHER

Bannerstone House

301-327 East Lawrence Avenue, Springfield, Illinois, U.S.A.

©1981 *by* CHARLES C THOMAS • PUBLISHER

ISBN 0-398-04463-5 cloth
ISBN 0-398-04464-3 paper

Library of Congress Catalog Card Number: 80-29434

*With THOMAS BOOKS careful attention is given to all details of manufacturing and de-
sign. It is the Publisher's desire to present books that are satisfactory as to their physical
qualities and artistic possibilities and appropriate for their particular use. THOMAS
BOOKS will be true to those laws of quality that assure a good name and good will.*

Library of Congress Cataloging in Publication Data

Shapiro, Constance Hoenk.
    Adolescent pregnancy prevention.

    Bibliography: p.
    Includes index.
    1. Birth Control--United States. 2. Pregnancy, Adolescent--
United States. 3. Sex instruction--United States. I. Title. [DNLM:
1. Pregnancy in adolescence. 2. Community--Institutional relations.
3. Schools. 4. Sex Education. WS 462 S529a]
HQ766.5.U5S52   363.9'6'088055   80-29434
ISBN 0-398-04463-5
ISBN 0-398-04464-3 (pbk.)

Printed in the United States of America
AF-R-1

TO STUART

PREFACE

Two-thirds of the one million pregnancies that occur to adolescents ✓ each year are unintended, and about half of teen pregnancies result in the births of unplanned children.[1] Moreover, the suicide rate for adolescent mothers is ten times that of the total population.[2]

For many years the focus of educators and helping professionals has been on the pregnant adolescent or the single teenage mother. This perspective has neglected entirely a preventive approach to the problem of adolescent pregnancy. Somehow it is more possible for adults to deal with the reality of a pregnant adolescent rather than to acknowledge the emerging sexuality of young people, male and female alike.

My interest in adolescent pregnancy prevention stems from ten years of experience as a social worker with pregnant and sexually active adolescents in school settings, residential treatment centers, child guidance centers, and probation departments. The concept of this book has emerged from my efforts as consultant to numerous family planning agencies, co-investigator of a grant on adolescent pregnancy prevention, instructor at in-service training sessions for educators and community professionals across New York State, and leader of seminars in human sexuality at Cornell University. The emphasis on a cooperative approach to school-community adolescent pregnancy prevention fills a gap in the literature on this topic. A preliminary monograph of this book entitled *Adolescent Pregnancy Prevention: A Team Approach* has been distributed nationwide to medical professionals, educators, religious leaders and community residents concerned with the serious consequences of unprotected sexual activity among adolescents.

Correspondence with many of these readers indicates that they perceive a need for school and community programs on sexual learning but are uncertain where to begin, how to deal with resistance, and with whom to generate cooperative working relationships. My purpose in writing this book is to highlight for concerned parents, teachers, religious leaders, family planners, and other helping professionals the dimensions and ramifications of adolescent sexual activity and to suggest some broad-based school and community responses to the prevention of

[1] Alan Guttmacher Institute. *11 Million Teenagers*. New York: Planned Parenthood Federation of America, Inc., 1976.
[2] S. Gordon. "Family Planning Education for Adolescents." Paper presented for the Commission on Population Growth and the American Future, 1972.

adolescent pregnancy.

Professional colleagues from academia and from community settings have provided much support, encouragement, and constructive criticism in the preparation of this book. I owe particular thanks to Cornell colleagues David Deshler, John Ford, Dennis Ritchie, and Ruth Stock Zober. The contributions from David Connor and Mary Kuhr have sensitized me to community issues and dilemmas facing persons in the helping professions. Devora Johnson deserves special appreciation for her patient efforts in typing the final manuscript.

C.H.S.

INTRODUCTION

Public attitudes toward adolescent pregnancy have changed in the past generation from an effort to ignore and deny the problem to one of dealing with it more openly, although the focus is still more on interventions and programs for pregnant adolescent females than on prevention. This is typical of society's attitudes toward adolescent sexuality — that it deserves attention only when it presents problems. Another bias is the inordinate focus on programs for adolescent females, to the exclusion of their male counterparts. Yet males share equally in creating the condition of pregnancy and, in some cases, carry even greater responsibility for having persuaded their reluctant female partners to engage in intercourse.

Prevention of adolescent pregnancy should not be targeted at female adolescents alone, nor should it be limited to the adolescent years. Adults and children alike need more attention in the area of improved sexual learning. In order to provide children and adolescents with the support they need in developing their sexual identities, many adults in the community will need to reshape the thinking about their roles as providers of sexual learning.

This book emphasizes the importance of school and community involvement in efforts at adolescent pregnancy prevention. One thread throughout the book is that sexual learning occurs throughout the life cycle in a wide range of different environments. Yet the quality and accuracy of existing opportunities for sexual learning are woefully inadequate in most communities. Whereas in the past, parents, schools, community agencies, and religious organizations have often disputed whose role it is to provide sexual learning for youth, this book highlights the importance of sharing the task among the many environments in which sexual learning, albeit inadequate, is already occurring. The challenge faced in the homes, the schools, the religious organizations, the community and among young people themselves is to improve the quality of factual knowledge, skills, and resources so that young people may feel more comfortable accepting their sexuality as an integral part of their developing identities.

Sexual learning traditionally has been presented in a cursory fashion, when it is provided at all. Whether it is a brief unit in a school curriculum, a hurried parent-to-child presentation at the onset of puberty, a riculum, a hurried parent-to-child presentation at the onset of puberty, a passing reference to biblical scriptures, or a busy visit to a clinic, few potential learning environments have made a careful effort to relate to sexuality as one integral part of the young person's total identity. Research cited by Chilman (1980) shows that sexual behaviors are linked to such factors as levels of self-esteem, ego strength, a sense of personal competence, anxiety reactions, interpersonal attitudes and skills, family relationships, personal and familial values and expectations, stage of development, attitudes toward society, membership in social reference groups, life situation, the quality of relationships with members of the same and opposite sex, and the availability of birth control services. These findings suggest that the narrow approach to sexual learning adopted in so many schools and communities falls far short of the needs of young people and the adults who support their psychosocial development.

The many interrelated causes of adolescent pregnancy prevent any one response from being sufficient to reduce the increasing rate of out-of-wedlock births. In fact, although a united school-community approach will undoubtedly make impressive gains in the quality of new and existing programs, such an approach still will not eliminate some causal factors like poverty and high youth unemployment, with their roots in the larger society. However, hopefully schools and communities will find that efforts to improve sexual learning will extend beyond the stated goal of reducing adolescent pregnancies. Anticipated benefits of improved school-community programs may include parents who are more comfortable with their roles as sex educators of their children, religious leaders who are more able to provide counsel and guidance regarding sexual matters to members of their congregations, teachers who are able at all grade levels to integrate age-appropriate material about sexuality into the curriculum, medical and social agencies that are as attuned to prevention as to intervention, and young people who are more able to communicate with one another and to identify supports and resources in their quests for an integrated sexual self.

This book emphasizes the common challenges faced by members of the community when contemplating efforts at adolescent pregnancy prevention. Chapter One provides an overview of potential community response to the various needs demonstrated by today's youth. A wide awareness of the environments in which sexual learning occurs is presented, along with ideas for innovative and traditional programs designed to enhance both sexual learning and self-esteem.

Although Chapter Two is primarily concerned with the lack of attention to males in efforts at adolescent pregnancy prevention, the shared needs of their female counterparts are also presented in an effort to encourage an upgrading of sexual learning opportunities for both sexes.

Chapter Three identifies the special needs of another group traditionally shortchanged in sexual learning: the disabled adolescent. Drawing parallels between disabled youth and their non-disabled peers, the chapter highlights the common needs shared by both groups while at the same time presenting specific suggestions for programs relevant to young people with disabilities.

Chapter Four stresses the crucial importance of involving young people in the provision of services and programs for their peers. Utilizing the strengths of the peer network during adolescence, the program suggestions in this chapter can be adapted for either school or community agency use.

Chapter Five reviews the life cycle challenges facing many parents at the same time their children are reaching adolescence. Specific ideas for developing and conducting parent groups are presented with a focus on parental needs for knowledge, values, and communication techniques.

Chapter Six focuses on the role of the clergy in providing guidance to members of their congregations on sexual concerns. Acknowledging that religious leaders may feel most comfortable when utilizing community experts on human sexuality, the chapter suggests a variety of ways for religious institutions to become active in community efforts to improve the quality of sexual learning.

Chapter Seven anticipates that any community will need guidelines in order to develop a coherent school-community plan for improving existing programs and for establishing new efforts. Community resistance, the function of advisory groups, and the steps in program planning and program development are presented in an effort to help concerned school and community participants in their organizational efforts.

Chapter Eight (with Rosalind Kenworthy as co-author) is intended primarily to bolster the knowledge base of school and community members who wish to develop their expertise on topics relating to birth control and sexually transmitted diseases.

Each chapter contains a list of resource materials that interested readers may wish to utilize for a more in-depth exploration of the chapter's topic.

The appendix contains an annotated list of audiovisual resources on a wide range of topics covered within this book. Readers are urged to preview all audiovisual resources in order to determine their suitability for the target audience.

It is hoped that readers will utilize this book as a resource and as a catalyst for developing and expanding the opportunities for sexual learning in their schools and communities. Cooperation between both school and community, although time consuming and demanding, is crucial to any sustained and comprehensive effort in adolescent pregnancy prevention.

REFERENCES

Chilman, C.S. *Adolescent Sexuality in a Changing American Society*. Bethesda, Maryland: Center for Population Research, 1980.

CONTENTS

ADOLESCENT PREGNANCY PREVENTION

CHAPTER 1

SEXUAL LEARNING AND SELF-ESTEEM

Adolescent pregnancy is not a new concern in the United States; however, the dimensions are shifting rapidly as more unmarried adolescents are choosing to keep their babies (94%) and as teenagers are sexually active and become pregnant at earlier ages than in previous generations. The rate of births to adolescents ages 16 to 19 has actually decreased, while the largest increase in pregnant teenagers is among the 13, 14, and 15-year olds (Chilman, 1979). In part, the increased birth rate among young teens is due to the earlier onset of menses and more adequate nutritional habits than a generation ago. Clearly, too, involvement in sexual activity at increasingly younger ages contributes to greater risk of pregnancy.

The Alan Guttmacher Institute (1976) estimated that *half* of the nearly 4 million sexually active teenage females in the United States and *most* of the 7 million sexually active teenage males have never made use of professional birth control services. Chilman (1979) reports that it is common for teenage girls to be sexually active for a year or more before they seek help in obtaining contraceptives — an indicator that the availability of contraceptives does not stimulate adolescents to participate in coitus. In fact, it is apparent that the younger the adolescents are when engaging in sexual activity the less knowledge they are likely to be about protecting themselves against unwanted pregnancies. Rarely is sex education provided early enough in a young person's life to serve a preventive function. Rather than waiting until burgeoning sexuality presents the potential for problems in adolescence, parents and community educators should support early and ongoing sexual learning for children of all ages. If children perceive sexuality as an integral part of their identities from the youngest years, then they can be encouraged toward responsible decision making as they reach sexual maturity.

Clearly, abstinence from sexual activity is one choice available to young people. However, despite most adults' encouragement that adolescents refrain from sexual activity, efforts at adolescent pregnancy prevention must also emphasize the importance of contraception for those young males and females who choose to be sexually active.

Adolescent pregnancy presents risks in terms of health, education, employment, and family stability. The most comprehensive efforts to prevent adolescent pregnancy must involve many sectors of the community, working together to pool expertise and to create an environment in which young people can learn about responsible sexual behavior.

A Community Perspective

Although concerned adults are overwhelmingly united in their agreement that the prevention of adolescent pregnancy is desirable, there is less consensus on the kinds of efforts that will serve to accomplish this goal. Parents clamor that they should be the primary sex educators of their children, yet studies show that most parents are reluctant to talk with their children about issues relating to sexuality. In survey after survey, it has been found that fewer than 20 percent of young people today believe their parents gave them a satisfactory sex education (Gordon, Scales, and Everly, 1979). Fathers, in particular, are perceived as contributing minimally to their children's sex education. This is unfortunate not only for their sons but also for their daughters, who are interested in a male perspective on sexual issues and behaviors.

Advocates of presenting education in the schools meet with resistance from school administrators who fear widespread community disapproval; in fact this fear is largely unfounded. Scales (1979) reports that around the country less than 3 percent of parents have refused to allow their children to participate in a sex education program, and frequently parents end up requesting their own sex education. However, the availability of sex education varies greatly in quality and comprehensiveness. As illustrated in Figure 1, only two states require that sex education of some sort be taught. Many school districts that permit sex education explicitly prohibit information about contraception from being included (Kirby, Alter, and Scales, 1979).

Figure 2 shows the extent of parental and community involvement in planning for sex education instruction in various states (Kirby, Alter, and Scales, 1979). Unfortunately, excluding parents and community

2

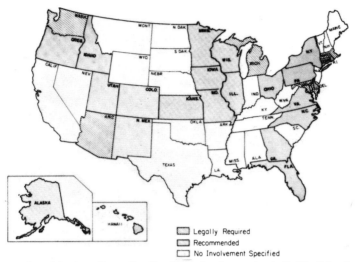

Legally Required
Recommended
No Involvement Specified

Figure 1. State Mandates Regarding Sex Education Instruction in Public Schools.

persons from the planning process often heightens their resistance to incorporating sex education into the academic curriculum of local public schools.

The typical educational approach is not to introduce sex education until junior or senior high school and then to restrict it to a presentation of reproductive functioning, usually as a unit in a health course. Such a focus on "plumbing" clearly omits many areas of concern to adolescents, such as self-image, sexual attraction, emotional attachments, and peer pressure.

Family planners assert that greater availability of birth control devices and information is needed, yet other experts point out that few methods of birth control are really suited to the teenager whose sexual encounters are often unplanned and sporadic. Furthermore, adolescent males often find that family planning clinics are not designed to meet their needs. When males are confronted with an all female staff, posters on the wall that relate to women's issues and literature focusing predominantly on women's health care, they are often discouraged from seeking services. Some changes are being made so that males feel less alienated as consumers of family planning services, but clearly these changes must be pursued vigorously.

Religious leaders deplore the lack of attention to moral and ethical

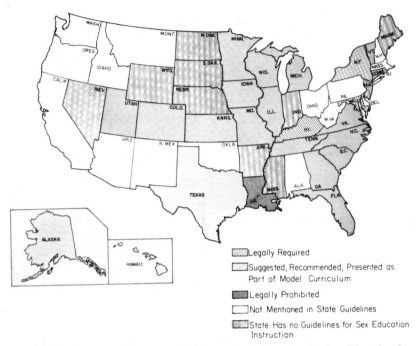

Legally Required

Suggested, Recommended, Presented as Part of Model Curriculum

Legally Prohibited

Not Mentioned in State Guidelines

State Has no Guidelines for Sex Education Instruction

Figure 2. Involvement of Parents and Community in Planning for Sex Education Instruction in Public Schools.

issues in community sex education efforts, yet many are reluctant to initiate programs within their congregations to deal with young people's concerns about their sexuality. One outstanding feature of those denominations that have developed a sex education curriculum is the emphasis on parents and children learning and talking together about sexual issues. Since adolescents consistently express disappointment that their parents are not more active contributors to their sexual learning, it makes sense for sex education programs to facilitate this communication process whenever possible. Religious organizations are an ideal setting for this to occur, as many parents feel strongly that they need support in their efforts to communicate about the moral and ethical components of sexual expression.

Researchers identify multiple factors that contribute to adolescent pregnancy: some teens are ignorant of factual information about reproduction and contraception; some are reluctant to protect themselves against pregnancy because they are ambivalent about themselves as sexual beings (they don't want to seem as if they are prepared for, or expecting to have, sex); some do not discuss birth control with their partners, which results in some couples having unprotected or "underprotected" intercourse; and, finally, some actively desire parenthood, believing that it will bring rewards and satisfaction lacking in current family, education, employment, and social experiences.

Because there is no one single factor associated with adolescent pregnancy, it is unrealistic to seek a single solution. Yet any comprehensive approach must deal with both factual and affective components.

Sexual Learning

One approach that incorporates a broad perspective is the concept of sexual learning. Although highly applicable to adolescent pregnancy prevention, sexual learning strives for a broader goal of helping persons at all stages of the life cycle become comfortable with their sexuality. Sexual learning is broader than sex education in that it includes the acquisition of attitudes, values, and behaviors as well as information. Sexual learning takes place from infancy through old age and can occur in a wide range of environments. If we accept the broadened notion of sexual learning in place of the more narrow concept of sex education, a wide range of learning efforts could be encouraged in such areas as: (1) *Communication Skills* between parents and children, teachers and students, clergy and congregation, and between sexual partners; (2) *Decision-Making Skills* which help youth to cope with peer pressure, exploitive relationships, confusing media messages, and efforts at autonomy from parents; (3) *Knowledge of Factual Information* about sexuality and its relevance to one's own life, with consideration for interests and needs at specific stages of the life cycle; and (4) *Values,* whether the emphasis is on acquisition or re-evaluation, youth and adults need moral and ethical benchmarks to guide their actions and decisions. Included in this should be attention to sex role stereotyping, which so frequently influences sexual behavior and relationships.

Parents and community members often fear that for young people to have knowledge about sex will cause them to have sexual experiences they wouldn't otherwise have. Yet, adults must realize that teenagers are

5

increasing their sexual learning by a variety of means. Those who do not have access to informed and "askable" adults will rely on their peers and the media for knowledge — both are sources regarded as highly unreliable and inaccurate by most adults. Research cited by Gordon, Scales, and Everly (1979) shows that teenagers who have talked to their parents about sex tend to delay first intercourse and then to use contraception when they do become sexually active.

Once we have accepted that accurate knowledge about sexuality does not lead to promiscuity and that many kinds of knowledge are relevant to the concept of sexual learning, we can appreciate the inappropriateness of "turf-guarding" by individuals or community groups.

Since sexual learning occurs in many environments throughout the life cycle, an important focus in any community should be on improving the accuracy and quality of information about sexuality. Parents, nursery school staff, youth group leaders, extension agents, coaches, medical professionals, teachers, clergy, and social service providers should work cooperatively toward becoming more knowledgeable and more comfortable with their roles as potential sex educators.

Young people who have been encouraged to take an active and responsible role in their own learning have found a number of creative ways to obtain and to share accurate information. Peer education and peer counseling groups, although not exclusively focused on sexual issues, recognize that many concerns expressed by adolescents relate to their sexuality. Peer counselors are trained to provide accurate information, appropriate referrals, and peer support for responsible behavior. Scales (1979) reports that the National Alliance for Optional Parenthood (NAOP) is interested in working with the high school press. Since advertising research indicates that more than 90 percent of high school students read their school papers, NAOP is encouraging students to write articles on sexuality, pregnancy, and teenage parenthood for their newspapers.

An imaginative approach to communicating with young people about common adolescent concerns is through theater groups. Teenage actors develop short skits portraying issues such as parent-child relationships, drugs, sexuality, authority, and other interpersonal concerns. The discussion period following each skit enables the audience to question the actors while they remain in character or to respond to questions posed by

6

the moderator. Theater groups provide performances in a variety of community settings upon request: schools, religious institutions, PTA's, and youth groups. The realistic protrayal of human dilemmas, options, and consequences provokes members of the audience to contemplate the relevance of the skits to their own lives.

Self-Esteem

Sexual learning, although an important component of any effort at adolescent pregnancy prevention, does not sufficiently address the needs of those adolescents who choose parenthood because they believe it holds more satisfactions than their current lives of school failure, unemployment, family discord, and social isolation. For some adolescents who feel little sense of opportunity, having babies becomes the best way to define positive roles for themselves in society. Building self-esteem is a critical component in preventing adolescent pregnancies. Adolescents who feel positively about themselves are not as likely to participate in exploitive relationships or to take a fatalistic approach to their future.

The educational system can have an impact on increasing the self-esteem of today's youth. Children and adolescents with learning problems need enriched educational opportunities; parents need to be more actively involved in the schools; youth with social and emotional problems need to rely on improved staffing for such student services as school social work, guidance counseling, school psychology, and school health services in elementary schools as well as in the higher grades. In general, students need to feel that success in school can lead to productive adult roles, particularly in terms of work and employment. The most common reason given in a recent New York City study of 1000 adolescents (Ross, 1979) for use of contraception was the desire to finish one's education. If the best users of contraception have personal goals and are committed to the pursuit of these goals, vocational education and employment programs for young people may be an effective way to prevent adolescent pregnancy.

The adolescents in the New York City study cited ''getting a job I enjoy'' as their most important priority. To the extent that, in this society, a person's self-esteem and value to others is related to wage

7

earning, it is possible to understand why teens, discouraged by high youth unemployment and inadequate vocational preparation, engage in behavior that adults consider counterproductive. For unemployed adolescents, parenthood may seem like one of the few available roles in which they can demonstrate competence and responsible behavior. High emphasis should be placed on programs that place adolescents in work situations that teach them the decision-making and technical skills necessary for independence and responsible participation in today's society.

Adolescence is a difficult developmental stage for the individual and the family. Community supports for troubled families can enable family members to improve communication, negotiate conflicts, clarify realistic expectations, and seek more mutually satisfying roles as changes occur within the family unit. Individual and family counseling can be a method of enhancing self-esteem and reducing the need of the adolescent to perceive pregnancy as an opportunity to escape from a stressful family unit.

The media has the capacity to communicate messages that influence self-esteem. Children and adolescents, as impressionable consumers, are greatly influenced by songs, television programs, advertisements, magazines, and movies that portray macho men, women as mindless sex objects, and relationships based on cat-and-mouse games rather than relationships based on mutual caring, trust, equality and open communication.

The compelling problem of adolescent pregnancy demands community responses that reflect cooperation, not competition, between diverse community elements such as: youth, parents, clergy, schools, youth employment agencies, social service providers, and medical professionals. The intertwined needs for sexual learning and self-esteem do not orginate in adolescence but, rather, are present throughout the life cycle. To have an impact on the sexual behavior and contraceptive practices of teenagers, programs must be developed not just for teenagers, but also for those adults who wish to be more involved in increasing the sexual learning of young people today.

References

Alan Guttmacher Institute. *11 Million Teenagers*. New York: Planned Parenthood Federation of America, Inc., 1976.

Chilman, C.S. Teenage pregnancy: a research review. *Social Work, 24:*492-498, 1979.

Gordon, S., Scales, P., and Everly, K. *The Sexual Adolescent*. North Scituate, Massachusetts: Duxbury Press, 1979.

Kirby, D., Alter, J., and Scales, P. *An Analysis of U.S. Education Programs and Evaluation Methods*. Bethesda, Maryland: Mathtech, Inc., 1979.

Ross, S. *The Youth Values Project*. Washington, D.C.: The Population Institute, 1979.

Scales, P. The context of sex education and the reduction of teen-age pregnancy. *Child Welfare, 58:*263-273, 1979.

Resource Materials

For Young Children

Andry, A.C., and Kratka, S. *Hi, New Baby*. New York: Simon and Schuster, 1970. Grades 1-3.

Andry, A.C., and Schepp, S. *How Babies are Made*. New York: Time-Life Books, 1968. Grades 5-6.

Arnstein, H.S. *Billy and our New Baby*. New York: Behavioral Publications, 1973. Grades K-2.

De Schweinitz, K. *Growing Up, How We Become Alive, are Born and Grow*. New York: Collier Books, 1974. Grades K-2.

Ets, M. *The Story of a Baby*. New York: Viking Press, Inc., 1969. Grades K-2.

Gordon, S., and Gordon, J. *Did the Sun Shine Before You Were Born?* New York: Third World Press, 1974. Grades K-2.

Gordon, S. *Girls are Girls and Boys are Boys – so What's the Difference?* Charlottesville, Virginia: Ed-U-Press, 1974. Grades K-3.

Gruenberg, S. *The Wonderful Story of How You Were Born*. New York: Doubleday and Company, Inc., 1973.

Mayle, P. *Where Did I Come From?* Secaucus, New Jersey: Lyle Stuart, Inc., 1973. Grades K-3.

Nilsson, L. *How Was I Born?* New York: Delacorte Press, 1975. Grades K-6.

Waxman, S. *What is a Girl? What is a Boy?* Culver City, California: Peace Press, 1976. Grades K-3.

For Pre- and Young Adolescents

Beck, L.F. *Human Growth, the Story of How Life Begins and Goes On*. New York: Harcourt Brace Jovanovich, 1969. Grades 6-9.

Duvall, E. *About Sex and Growing Up*. New York: Associated Press, 1968. Grades 6-8.

Gordon, S. *Facts about Sex for Today's Youth*. Charlottesville, Virginia: Ed-U-Press, 1978. Grades 5-7.

Hofstein, S., and Bauer, W.W. *The Human Story*. Glenview, Illinois: Scott, Foresman and Company, 1977. Grades 5-7.

Johnson, C.B., and Johnson, E.W. *Love and Sex and Growing Up*. Philadelphia : J.B. Lippincott Company, 1977. Grades 6-9.

Lerrigo, M., and Cassidy, M. *A Doctor Talks to 9-12-Year-Olds*. Chicago: Budlong Press, 1974. Grades 5-7.

Lerrigo, M., and Southard, H. *A Story About You: Facts You Want to Know About Sex*. Chicago: American Medical Association, 1969. Grades 6-7.

Levine, M., and Seligman, J. *A Baby is Born*. New York: Simon and Schuster, 1969. Grades 6-7.

Lyman, M. *Growing up – Especially for Pre-teens and Young Teens*. Syracuse, New York: Planned Parenthood Center of Syracuse, 1973. Grades 5-7.

May, J. *How We are Born*. Chicago: Follett Publishing Co., 1969. Grades 6-9.

May, J. *Men and Women*. Chicago: Follett Publishing Co., 1969. Grades 5-7.

Mayle, P. *What's Happening to Me?* Secaucus, New Jersey: Lyle Stuart, 1975. Grades 5-7.

Strain, F.B. *Being Born*. New York: Hawthorne Books, Inc., 1970. Grades 6-7.

For Adolescents

Burn, H. *Better than the Birds, Smarter than the Bees*. Nashville, Tennessee: Abington Press, 1969. Grades 7-12.

Dalrymple, W. *Sex for Real: Human Sexuality and Sexual Responsibility*. New York: McGraw-Hill Book Co., 1969. Grades 9-12.

Demarest, R., and Sciarra, J. *Conception, Birth and Contraception*. New York: McGraw-Hill Book Co., 1969. Grades 9-12.

Dolloff, P.B., and Resnick, M. *Patterns of Life: Human Growth and Development*. Columbus, Ohio: Charles E. Merrill Publishing Co., 1972. Grades 9-12.

Duvall, E. *Love and the Facts of Life*. New York: Associated Press, 1968. Grades 9-12.

Gordon, S. *Facts About Sex*. Charlottesville, Virginia: Ed-U-Press, 1978. Grades 9-12.

Gordon, S. *You Would if You Loved Me*. New York: Bantam Books, 1978, Grades 7-12.

Gordon, S., and Conant, R. *You – a Survival Guide for Young People*. New York: Quadrangle/The New York Times Book Company, Inc., 1975. Grades 10-12.

Hamilton, E. *Sex with Love: A Guide For Young People*. Boston: Beacon Press, 1978. Grades 7-9.

Hettlinger, R.F. *Growing Up With Sex*. New York: The Seabury Press, Inc., 1971. Grades 10-12.

Johnson, E. *Love and Sex in Plain Language*. Philadelphia: J.B. Lippincott Co., 1977. Grades 7-12.

Johnson, E.W. *Sex: Telling it Straight*. New York: Bantam Books, Inc., 1971. Grades 7-9.

Julian, C. J., and Jackson, E. N. *Modern Sex Education*. New York: Holt, Rinehart and Winston, Inc., 1972. Grades 10-12.

Kelly, G.F. *Learning About Sex – The Contemporary Guide for Young Adults*. New York: Barron's Educational Series, Inc., 1976. Grades 9-12.

Kelman, P., and Saxon, B. *Modern Human Sexuality*. Boston: Houghton Mifflin Company, 1979. Grades 9-12.

Lyman, M. *Teen Questions About Sex – and Answers*. Syracuse, New York: Planned Parenthood Center of Syracuse, 1973. Grades 7-9.

Nelson, J. *Teenagers and Sex: Revolution or Reaction,* Englewood Cliffs, New Jersey: Prentice-Hall, 1970. Grades 9-12.

Mazur, R. M. *Commonsense Sex*. Boston: Beacon Press, 1973. Grades 10-12.

Power, J. *How Life Begins*. New York: Simon and Schuster, Inc., 1968. Grades 6-12.

Riker, A.P., and Riker, C. *Finding My Way*. Peoria, Illinois: Charles A. Bennett, Co., Inc., 1979. Grades 8-12.

Southard, H.F., *Sex Before Twenty: New Answers for Young People*. New York: E.P. Dutton and Co., 1971. Grades 10-12.

What Teens Want to Know But Don't Know How to Ask. New York: Planned Parenthood Federation of America, Inc., 1976. Grades 7-9.

Whelan, E. *Sex and Sensibility: A New Look at Being a Woman*. New York: McGraw-Hill Book Company, 1974. Grades 10-12.

Winship, E.C., and Caparulo, F. *Masculinity and Feminity*. Boston: Houghton Mifflin Co., 1978. Grades 10-12.

Voelckers, E. *Girls' Guide to Menstruation*. New York: Rosen Press, 1975. Grades 7-12.

11

CHAPTER 2

THE MALE AS AN AFTERTHOUGHT IN SEX EDUCATION EFFORTS

Adolescent males and females are equally in need of improved sexual learning. Increasingly, sex education classes and programs are designed for a coeducational audience, which gives males and females an opportunity to become comfortable learning and discussing together a range of concerns related to the sexuality of persons of both sexes. However, in many communities and school systems, public concern with teenage sexuality has most frequently focused on the teenage female. Although the role of the adolescent male is occasionally acknowledged in literature on sexual learning, he is still an afterthought in many programs concerned with human sexuality. For this reason, it seems that a special emphasis on the male's need for sex education is warranted.

The Existing Ecological Context

Recent studies show that parents support the schools' efforts to offer sex education in their curricula (Scales, 1978; Rensberger, 1978). Yet, many parents feel strongly that primary responsibility for sex education begins in the home, despite evidence that parents are reluctant to discuss sexual matters with their children. Lacking the knowledge and vocabulary to discuss sexuality, some parents avoid any opportunities to help their growing children learn about their sexuality. By their teen years many adolescents may have given up on seeking information on sexuality from their parents. Likewise, the longer parents delay before encouraging discussion of sexual matters at home, the more awkward they feel communicating information and value stances to their adolescent. Even for parents who are able to discuss some sexual matters with their children, the range of topics is often narrow. In a study by Roberts, Kline, and Gagnon (1978) of over 1,400 Cleveland, Ohio parents, between 85 and 95 percent of all parents interviewed said they had *never* mentioned any aspect of erotic behavior (e.g. intercourse, premarital sex) or its social consequences (e.g. pregnancy, venereal disease, contraception, and abortion) to their children.

Limited data are available on parents' efforts to discuss sexuality with their sons. The 1978 study of Cleveland parents revealed that less than 2 percent of fathers and only 9 percent of mothers had discussed premarital sex with their sons. A study by Paonessa and Paonessa (1971) of 127 parents enrolled in a series of lectures on sex education revealed that 53 percent of mothers believed that their sons had been prepared for nocturnal emissions. Most of these women stated that their husbands had given their sons the information, but only 9 percent of the fathers stated that they had prepared their sons. Regrettably, fathers are less involved than mothers in the sex education of their offspring. Yet it is the father who has the unique potential to be most reassuring to his son in preparing him for spontaneous erections, wet dreams, and other physical changes occurring at puberty. The father also needs to be aware of his influence in the area of sexual values, since peers and the media will have begun already to influence his son's attitudes in a wide range of areas relating to sexuality.

The more opportunities that both parents, including the father, can take to correct mistaken impressions and distorted values, the more able their offspring are to discriminate between biased and inaccurate information. Clearly this presumes a mutual willingness for parents and children to communicate and, if this has not developed comfortably over the years, the parents may need to find creative ways of bridging the communication gap. If the gap remains, then young people are free to draw their own conclusions about parental beliefs and attitudes.

Often as influential as what is discussed openly are adolescent assumptions about parental attitudes. A double standard emerges in the Youth Values Project, a 1979 study of 1,000 New York City adolescents by Ross. When asked how their mothers would respond to learning of their children's sexual activity, 41 percent of the adolescent females anticipated that their mothers would "be very upset" as opposed to 28 percent of the males. When questioned about their fathers' response, 45 percent of the females stated that their fathers would "be very upset," compared with 22 percent of the males. It is striking that 65 percent of the males surveyed in the Youth Values Project anticipated their fathers would have either neutral (e.g. "not care") or positive reactions (e.g.

13

''say it's normal'') to learning of their sons' sexual activity. Only 7 percent of the males anticipated their fathers would suggest birth control. This is of particular concern in light of Furstenberg's findings (1976) that usually female adolescents and their mothers expected the male to assume responsibility for ''using protection.'' An earlier study by Arnold (1973) supports these findings. In a survey of males participating in a condom distribution program, Arnold found that only 15 percent of the program's condom recipients indicated that their partners were independently using contraception, leading to the strong suspicion that adolescent males are generally expected by their sexual partners to assume the major responsibility for contraception. Yet males surveyed by the Youth Values Project (Ross, 1979) were uniformly less knowledgeable than females about all forms of birth control. Fewer than half of the sexually active males indicated they had ''heard a lot about the condom'' which clearly suggests that greater familiarity with this and other forms of birth control is needed.

Young males who perceive the message from their parents that sowing their wild oats is an expected rite of passage to adulthood are entitled to more clear information about the responsibilities accompanying sexual activity, namely: use of birth control, avoidance of exploitation, respect for the relationship, protection and check-ups against sexually transmitted diseases, and consideration for one's sexual partner. Parents should also be sensitive to the double standard that they convey regarding the sexual behavior of their sons and daughters. Adolescents have enough difficulties making responsible sexual decisions without having parentally conveyed sex role stereotypes foisted upon them.

Interestingly, the transformation in sex roles may be leading to a new phenomenon in adolescent relationships. Whereas in earlier years it was presumed that the female felt pressured to enter into a sexual relationship, this trend appears to be undergoing a change. One of the more surprising findings in the Youth Values Project (1979) was the response to the statement: ''On one or more occasions I've done sexual things mostly because the person I was with expected me to.'' As anticipated, the most frequent overall response was ''no.'' However, contrary to expectations, twice as great a percentage of the males as females felt they had responded to sexual pressure by their partner. This was a clear suggestion that much of teen males' sexual activity is caused by the expectations, or perceived expectations, of their partners, rather than of other males.

Certainly such findings should encourage the sex educator to be aware of the need males may feel for assertive training, improving communication skills with their female peers, and separating their sense of self-esteem from the machismo image they believe they are expected to convey. The use by males of Sol Gordon's book *You Would If You Loved Me* (1978) might enable some males to develop appropriate responses to unwelcome sexual overtures by their female peers.

However, regardless of who initiates sexual activity, the statistics of nonuse of birth control by sexually active couples are truly alarming. As shown in Table I, data from several studies on condom use by adolescents reveal that only a small percentage of teenage males regularly use the condom as a form of birth control. Sorensen (1973) reported that only a "small minority" of teenage males always know what method of birth control is being used and about one-fifth trusted luck to prevent pregnancy. Furthermore, males need more support from parents and educators in perceiving their role in unwanted pregnancies.

TABLE I

Condom Use by Adolescent Males

			Percent Who Use Condoms				
Study	**Geographic Sample**	**n**	**Always**	**Often**	**Sometimes**	**Rarely**	**Never**
Youth Values Project[a]	New York City	185	11	8	29	NA	51
The Male's Place[b]	Santa Clara Co., CA	100	15	3	15	11	56
Circus Magazine[c]	National	100	27	NA	30	NA	43
R.C. Sorensen[d]	National	198	15	11	17	NA	57

[a]Data From S. Ross, **The youth values project,** Washington, D.C.: The Population Institute, 1979, 24.

[b]Data from Combating 'street' information. **The Family Planner,** Spring, 1978, **9,** 13.

[c]Data compiled in Tapping the teen mood. **The Family Planner,** Spring, 1978, **9,** 6.

[d]Data from R.C. Sorensen. **Adolescent sexuality in contemporary America.** New York: The World Publishing Co., 1973, 445.

In the 1973 study by Sorensen, nearly 40 percent of the males said that

15

they never thought about the possibility of the female's becoming pregnant. When asked about a time frame limited to the "last month," only 51 percent of the males with recent intercourse experience, compared with 82 percent of the females, indicated that they had thought about whether or not the female might conceive.

Reasons most commonly cited in the Youth Values Project (1979) by males for contraceptive nonuse include: "It interferes with pleasure," "My partner doesn't like it," "It makes sex seem too planned," and "It is too embarrassing to buy."

Not all homes have a parent figure with whom the adolescent male is comfortable discussing sexual matters. In single parent homes headed by women, mothers may feel inadequate or awkward in meeting their sons' needs for sexual information. Some fathers are sufficiently uncomfortable with their roles in their sons' sex education that they neither initiate nor respond to opportunities for discussion.

In order to support the home as an environment where the adolescent can feel encouraged to discuss sexual matters, outreach and adult education efforts must focus on helping parents to gain factual information, to be more "askable," to be more comfortable in initiating discussions, and to acknowledge that their sons are just as much in need of guidance in sexual matters as are their daughters.

The schools are a second environment for primary prevention of adolescent pregnancy. Yet, because of a cautious attitude toward controversial topics, most schools still do not perform more than a rudimentary function in sex education. Although health and biology classes may choose to present information on human sexuality, this material is likely to focus exclusively on the anatomical, with little consideration for practical issues such as contraception or humanistic values concerned with sexual expression. Scales (1978) cites figures showing that approval of sex education in the school has increased 12 percent since 1970, with 77 percent now in favor of it, and those who approve of talking about birth control in school have increased dramatically from 36 percent in 1970 to 69 percent in 1978, with no difference between Catholics and non-Catholics. Yet there is still no requirement in nearly 90 percent of the states on teaching about birth control, abortion, feelings, and communication.

Family life education classes, often a module of home economics courses, have an excellent potential for incorporating material on human sexuality beyond the biological aspects. Yet these courses tend to attract female students in greater numbers than male students. A most important effect of expanded male enrollment might be the opportunity to learn with their female classmates about coping with peer pressure, heightened awareness of their sexuality, and responsible decision making.

At the present time, the television and the street corner provide at least as many opportunities as the school environment for males to learn with and from their peers about their developing sexuality. Yet television and peers are not thought by parents to be the most accurate sources of information. Adolescence is a time during which the peer group assumes an increasingly important function, as the adolescent tries out and discards different roles in the search for identity. Since peer groups take over some of the parental roles of furnishing support and values, their importance as a primary reference group must not be underestimated. Consolidating one's identity requires validation by peers of both sexes of the development of one's sexuality. If peers are influenced by television, sexually stereotyped parental messages, and incomplete factual information, they may be a source of mutual confusion rather than responsive support for their friends.

Community agencies, especially family planning agencies and public health departments, are a third environment in which primary prevention and sex education occur. Again, males often perceive that these agencies respond to the needs of their female peers more readily. Public health nurses and staffs of family planning clinics are overwhelmingly female; only recently have family planning clinics made a concerted effort to hire male workers. Unless specific outreach efforts are made to males, they will feel reluctant to seek out an agency so closely identified with providing services for females. Other community agencies serving adolescent males must be aware that although their reason for agency involvement may not relate overtly to sexual concerns, these concerns may be very close to the surface and should not be ignored if the adolescent acknowledges their relevance to his needs.

Religious institutions provide still another environment for sex education. Many denominations have developed educational programs for use by their priests, ministers, and rabbis. These programs, which emphasize the moral and ethical considerations in sexual activity, fre-

17

quently involve parents and are designed to address the needs of adolescent boys as well as girls. However, the existence of such programs does not insure their implementation on the local level. Religious leaders who perceive other priorities in their work may need encouragement from their congregations before allocating time and effort to sex education programs.

Despite the variety of learning environments in which adolescent males could receive knowledge about themselves as developing sexual persons, the majority of existing educational and preventive programs favor the needs of adolescent females. Such program priorities do not necessarily represent a wish to exclude males; rather, the priorities are indicative of the double standard still pervasive in our society — that since pregnancy has the greatest impact on the adolescent female, she alone must take responsibility for not becoming pregnant. In fact, pregnancy has many consequences for the putative fathers beyond serving as a confirmation of their virility. Some males leave school to seek employment so they can help to support the baby, some marry their pregnant partners, some disclaim responsibility for the pregnancy, some continue the relationship with the single mother and serve as a single father to their offspring. If the pregnancy is terminated, the putative father will feel the impact of this loss, according to a 1978 study by Horowitz.

Since efforts at sex education are frequently aimed at the teenage female, it is important to consider how the learning environments can be expanded to respond to the needs of the sexually maturing male.

Parent Groups

The availability of parent education groups can be helpful in several ways. First, parents need to confront the myth that talking with their children about sexuality stimulates their children to become sexually active. Second, parents need to review, refresh, and correct their own factual knowledge about sexuality. Since few of today's parents received formal sex education, and since their own parents may not have been helpful role models as sex educators, parents may appreciate reading materials that they can review before initiating discussions with their children. Third, parents may need to enhance their communication

18

skills on sensitive issues that they are hesitant to discuss with their children. Modeling, role playing, and viewing films can serve to make parents more comfortable by expanding their repertoire of communication skills. Parents are often relieved to discover that they are not alone in their feelings of awkwardness. The camaraderie which develops in the group can result in an ongoing support system among the parents long after the group has formally terminated.

In order for parent groups to be successful in responding to the needs of adolescent males, it is especially important to include factual material and communication exercises which promote parents' comfort in talking openly with their sons. To whatever extent fathers can be encouraged to participate in parent groups, the greater the opportunity will be for them to gain comfort in responding to questions their sons prefer to discuss with a male. For the mother who is a single parent, or whose husband is uninvolved in discussing sexual matters with their children, a special effort should be made to help her be responsive to her sons. In addition, the mother may need help in identifying a male relative, teacher, or friend of the family who could share with her the responsibility for communicating both factual information and values about sexual matters to the sons in the family.

Perhaps most importantly, parents should be helped to feel comfortable in sharing with other community resources the effort to help their children become more aware and informed about their developing sexuality. Despite adult education and discussion groups, parents may still feel awkward in responding to all issues suggested by the burgeoning sexuality of their adolescents. By helping parents to do as much as they can manage comfortably, and to identify community resources to utilize as supports for themselves and their children, a helping professional can allay the guilt of those adults who feel inadequate at not being "super parents" in their function as sex educators.

The School

The school can be a solid community resource for expanding and developing sex education programs that respond to the needs of boys as well as girls. Health and biology teachers should be encouraged to move beyond the purely biological to include humanistic and ethical compo-

19

nents of reproduction and sexuality. Also, these teachers should be certain that students are able to understand the relevance of biological and anatomical information for themselves and their bodies. Mere attendance in a course or program that purports to teach sex education is no guarantee that students can apply the information presented to their own sexual situations. When the Youth Values Project (1979) surveyed 639 New York City adolescents, regardless of whether respondents obtained their information from a class in school, clinics, Planned Parenthood, magazines or books, only one-third of them knew when, during the menstrual cycle, conception is most likely to occur. In Finkel and Finkel's (1975) purposive sample of 400 urban high school males, only 32 percent knew that a female could get pregnant even if the male withdrew "before coming."

Teachers should be supported in their efforts to introduce material on responsible sexuality into their courses on family living, and family living courses should be designed with relevance for males and the responsibilities they will assume as young adults. Active outreach by teachers of family living courses to enroll male students is critical; it may be helpful to involve a male as a team teacher in certain segments of the family living course, thereby providing an adult role model for male students.

The concept of a teen counseling room is one which has been used in various ways in the schools. Outreach workers of family planning programs can staff a counseling room open for junior and senior high school students to visit during their study halls. Literature, models, samples, and films can be located in this room for use by the counselor or by teachers who teach sex education as part of their curricula. The outreach workers staffing the room provide information and referral services in addition to counseling adolescents on such topics as intimacy, birth control, sexuality, and relationship problems.

Community Agencies

In communities where local schools are not given the latitude to teach information on sexuality, community agencies can have an impact on adolescents. Youth bureaus and 4-H Clubs in some parts of the country have developed programs on teen sexuality for their members. Programs

20

in values clarification, decision making, and assertiveness training are appropriate for both adolescent males and females. Peer counseling groups, which can be organized and trained by local organizations, can have far reaching impact on adolescents in the community and in the schools. Because peer counselors are trained in outreach, rudimentary counseling techniques, and agency services relevant for teens, they are in an optimal position to provide emotional support for their friends as well as to facilitate a referral when more specialized information or counseling is needed.

Since family tensions, disappointing social relationships, or school failure may cause teens to consider escaping into premature marriage or parenthood, peer counselors can serve a critical function by suggesting supportive services or other alternatives for the troubled teen who is tempted to seek refuge in an untimely intimate relationship. Since adolescent males often have been socialized to believe that stoicism is equivalent to masculinity, peer counselors can be especially helpful in encouraging males to talk about their feelings, to recognize they are not alone in the problems they face, and to have a friend communicate caring and concern in addition to information and referral assistance. Since the peer group is such a powerful socializing agent among adolescents, peer counselors have the potential for being utilized more readily than some agency-based services.

Outreach attempts by family planning agencies need to be designed especially to attract teenagers. Agency hotlines appeal to teens because of their confidential, anonymous approach. Adolescents who have positive experiences in hotline conversations may feel more willing to come to the agency for counseling or an examination. Programs hoping to attract males must design publicity so that it is perceived as relevant to their needs. Posters and magazines in the waiting room should be of interest to males as well as females. Outreach workers should be accessible in locations where young males gather. Mobile units and trailers are ideal outreach vehicles that can be moved between shopping centers, sports facilities, libraries, and community centers. Such vehicles can also serve as a resource for parents, teachers, and religious leaders who may wish to borrow or become more familiar with materials available in the mobile unit.

Pregnancy counseling is an important time to try to involve the

21

adolescent male. Inasmuch as suspected pregnancy is viewed as a crisis by the female and her partner, the couple may be especially receptive to help and responsive to new learning. Although the fear of pregnancy is the initial catalyst for agency involvement, whatever the outcome the male should be encouraged to join his partner for contraceptive counseling.

Religious Institutions

Religious institutions having sexuality education programs frequently provide parallel involvement for parents and their adolescents. Parents are reassured that the curricula developed by religious denominations emphasize the moral and ethical dimension of sexuality in addition to factual information. Religious leaders who have not implemented such programs may need encouragement from their congregations or support from resource people in the community who are knowledgeable and comfortable presenting material on human sexuality to young people and their parents. Because the curricula developed under religious auspices are appropriate for males as well as females, teachers and teen leaders might want to review these materials as they develop their own programs.

Despite the potential for learning about human sexuality in the community, adolescent females are most frequently the primary targets in those sex education efforts that do exist. Most preventive efforts in adolescent pregnancy identify the female as the target when she seeks family planning services, when she enrolls in a family life education course, or when she actually becomes pregnant. The male is far more elusive as an identifiable target, since he can obtain contraceptives without seeing a physician and since many males do not perceive that existing services will meet their needs. Parental and community efforts at sex education must look beyond the common goal of pregnancy prevention to the expanded goal of helping adolescents to accept their sexuality as an integral component of their identity. Males deserve as much support as females, and all adolescents are entitled to more support from parents and community as they seek knowledge and values which can guide them in their efforts at responsible sexual intimacy. Since many adolescent boys will someday become fathers, it is hoped that a

22

comprehensive approach toward their present sex education may enable them to be more comfortable in the sex education of their future children than their own fathers have been with them.

REFERENCES

Arnold, C.B. A condom distribution program for adolescent males. In McCalister, D., Thiessen, V., and McDermott, M. (Eds.): *Readings in Family Planning*. St. Louis: The C.V. Mosby Company, 1973.

Finkel, M.L., and Finkel, D.J. Sexual and contraceptive knowledge, attitudes and behavior of male adolescents. *Family Planning Perspectives, 7*:256-260, 1975.

Furstenberg, F.F. *Unplanned Parenthood: The Social Consequences of Teenage Childbearing*. New York: The Free Press, 1976.

Gordon, S. *You Would If You Loved Me*. New York: Bantam Books, 1978.

Horowitz, N.H. Adolescent mourning reactions to infant and fetal loss. *Social Casework, 59*:551-559, 1978.

Paonessa, J.J. and Paonessa, M.W. The preparation of boys for puberty. *Social Casework, 52*:39-44, 1971.

Rensberger, B. Behavioral study indicates many parents don't tell children of erotic aspects of sex. *The New York Times*, Dec. 17, 1978, p. 30.

Roberts, E., Kline, D., and Gagnon, J. *Family Life and Sexual Learning: A Study of the Role of Parents in the Sexual Learning of Children*. Cambridge, Massachusetts: Population Education, Inc., 1978.

Ross, S. *The Youth Values Project*. Washington, D.C.: The Population Institute, 1979.

Scales, P. We are the majority — but who would know it? *Impact*, October, 1978, *1*:14-17.

Sorensen, R.C. *Adolescent Sexuality in Contemporary America*. New York: World, 1973.

Resource Materials

About Boys. Baltimore: Planned Parenthood.

A Boy Grows Up. Jefferson City, Missouri: Missouri Division of Health.

Brockman, F. *For Men Only*. New Orleans: Family Planning.

Gadpaille, W.J. *Father's Role in Sex Education of His Son*. Reprint available from Stanley Kruger, Special Programs Director, Bureau of School Systems, United States Office of Education, 400 Maryland Avenue, SW, Washington, D.C. 20202.

Julty, S. *Male Sexual Performance*. New York: Dell Books, 1975.

Julty, S. *Men's Bodies, Men's Selves*. New York: Dial Press, 1978.

Male Health Needs. Mount Pleasant, Michigan: Woman's Health and Information Project Box 110, Warriner Hall, CMU, 1975.

The Man's World: Sex Anatomy/Birth Control/V.D./the condom. New York: Population Services International, 1976.

Neft, M.G. *Focus on Health: The Male and Family Planning*. Bladensburg, Maryland: Westinghouse Learning Corporation, 1972.

Pomeroy, W.B. *Boys and Sex*. New York: Delacorte Press, 1970.

The Problem With Puberty. Denver: Rocky Mountain Planned Parenthood.

Roen, P.R. *Male Sexual Health*. New York: William Morrow and Co., 1974.

Whelan, S., and Whelan, E. *Making Sense Out of Sex: A New Look at Being a Man*. New York: McGraw-Hill Book Company, 1975.

Zilbergeld, B. *Male Sexuality: A Guide to Sexual Fulfillment*. Boston: Little, Brown and Company, 1978.

Zorabedian, T. *The View From Our Side: Sex and Birth Control for Men*. Atlanta: Family Planning Program, Emory University School of Medicine, 1977.

CHAPTER 3

THE DISABLED ADOLESCENT

The term, *disabled,* encompasses a wide range of individual differences and tends to call to mind inadequacies rather than capabilities. For this reason, some people find the term "disabled" to be offensive and stigmatizing. Yet it is critical to communicate the ways in which sexual learning can be made both relevant and accessible to persons with special needs. In this chapter, references to disabilities are intended to communicate distinctions in human capabilities and to emphasize the importance of individualizing for specific learning needs. Whenever possible, parallels between the needs of disabled and non-disabled individuals will be indicated.

In all areas of life, including the sexual sphere, disabled persons have a great deal in common with their non-disabled peers, yet labels and socialization experiences which occur in isolation from actual interaction with disabled persons have enabled stereotypes to develop. Such stereotypes often cause disabled persons to be disqualified from life experiences accorded their non-disabled peers. Worse still, some stereotypes promote the notion that all persons possessing a certain disability are identical in their needs. Fortunately, there is now an increasing recognition that, whether a person is identified as visually impaired, mentally retarded, hearing impaired, physically disabled, learning disabled, or emotionally disturbed, his/her capabilities and needs must be individually assessed, as there is wide variation in abilities identified by the same diagnostic label.

Young people who are disabled share with their non-disabled peers an interest in increasing their sexual learning. Other shared concerns during adolescence include gaining independence from their families, establishing rewarding peer relationships, exploring career possibilities, and consolidating their identities as young adults. In describing the needs for sexual learning faced by some disabled adolescents, Sol Gordon (1971) writes: "Yet exceptional children experience the same physical and

25

emotional changes that children do, as well as the same anxiety which often accompanies adolescence. Thus, they must cope with all the emotional conflicts of their normal teenage counterparts in addition to those produced by their handicaps.''

Sensitive adults must make every effort to individualize the needs of young people with disabilities, in order to maximize the opportunities they have for interacting with their non-disabled peers. Because social and educational mingling of disabled and non-disabled persons does not yet occur in as many circumstances as it could, adults must constantly make efforts to promote interaction between all adolescents in a wide range of environments. Social and educational isolation have especially deleterious effects on the sexual learning of adolescents with disabilities. Winifred Kempton (1975) identifies potential difficulties that young people may encounter, depending upon the nature of their disabilities and the responsiveness of others to their individual learning needs: "They have more difficulty in obtaining accurate information from their peers; they often do not know whom or what to ask; they have difficulty learning from books; and they are not able to learn easily from observing the behavior of others.''

Clearly, in many cases it is society and not the disability that cuts an adolescent off from important knowledge. Therefore, such barriers must be identified and confronted by parents, educators, and concerned community members. These barriers can be classified as attitudinal, social, and educational.

Attitudinal Barriers

First, it is relevant to acknowledge that community residents have mixed and often ambivalent attitudes toward sexual learning for all young people. On the one hand, adults fear that knowledge will lead young people to experiment with sexual behaviors in which they would not otherwise engage; on the other hand, skyrocketing adolescent pregnancy rates cause adults to believe that sexually active young people should have enough information to prevent unwanted pregnancies. Such ambivalent attitudes extend to the issue of sexual learning for young people with disabilities.

Although most parents experience some degree of awkwardness

26

when acknowledging their offsprings' sexuality, parents of disabled children face both their own hesitation and community ambivalence. Some parents anticipate the social rejection their children may encounter or foresee limited outlets for their expression of sexual feelings. In order to protect their children from disappointment, pain, and frustration, some parents ignore and stifle the sexual curiosity of their offspring in the hopes that an asexual existence will bring less pain than restless searches for sexual fulfillment. Other parents fear that their children will be exploited sexually. Young people who are especially trusting of adults, especially responsive to physical overtures, and eager to please may be highly vulnerable to sexual exploitation.

Some adults in the community are emphatically opposed to sexual learning by disabled individuals. Such adults refuse to believe that handicapped persons can live normal lives and they extend this prohibition to sexual expression. Other uninformed adults believe that disabled persons are asexual or they believe that so much effort must be spent in overcoming the disability that the person has little energy or interest left for sexual expression. Some community members express concerns that sexual learning may fuel an interest in marriage and families, which they see as responsibilities too burdensome for some disabled persons to bear. Attitudes regarding human sexuality tend to be different for mentally retarded individuals than for persons with other disabilities. A person with hearing or visual impairment generally is viewed as entitled to sexual fulfillment, marriage and childbearing, whereas much more disapproval surrounds the notion of a mentally retarded person pursuing such life roles.

However, discomfort in many communities is being offset and bolstered by the support networks that actively encourage persons with disabilities to lead fulfilling lives. Services such as employment counseling, financial assistance, medical care, and transportation can facilitate the movement of many disabled persons into the mainstream of community life. For these individuals, and for the adults who take pride and pleasure in their gains, the old taboos on sexual learning may disintegrate in the face of increasing competence in other spheres of their lives.

Not all disabled persons are able, even with supports, to lead lives comparable to those of non-disabled community residents. Yet, given

27

that all disabled persons are sexual beings, they should have access to opportunities for sexual learning that are individualized according to their abilities and readiness for such learning. Different levels of content, forms of presentation, methods of instruction, or social groupings can offer a wealth of educational possibilities for parents, teachers, and community members who acknowledge the sexuality of disabled youth.

Social Barriers

Social barriers are especially disadvantageous for disabled youth who, like their non-disabled peers, are trying to establish and consolidate their identities. Critical in this process is the opportunity to test out different roles, whether in the context of family relationships, work relationships, school relationships, or peer relationships. While adolescents are using their teen years to gain autonomy from their families and to consolidate peer relationships with acquaintances of both sexes, those with disabilities may face a special challenge in moving away from crucial family supports into a peer network that is uncertain how to include an adolescent with special needs. Family members must encourage and support this transition, as must other adults and young people who interact with disabled adolescents. James Maddock (1974) points out that this is especially important, given that many factors in the care and upbringing of disabled individuals may have interfered with opportunities to test out their autonomy gradually. He says: "With younger children, so much effort may be devoted to encouraging *individual* development that *interpersonal* development may be minimized. Even when exceptional children receive the best care and treatment, their involvement with adults may overshadow peer play opportunities. In particular, physical interaction between peers may suffer, apparently motivated by adult fears of either aggressive or sexual acting-out behavior."

Social barriers will differ somewhat, depending on the nature of the adolescent's disability. A disability requiring crutches, braces, or a wheelchair may hamper physical mobility or may discourage participation in certain popular teen activities, such as sports, dances, or hiking. Social awkwardness may accompany a visual or auditory impairment, which prevents the disabled adolescent from perceiving nuances, verbal

28

and non-verbal cues, and from participating in the easy banter of young people. Mental retardation and emotional disturbance vary in the extent to which social interaction is inhibited, but clearly self-esteem is affected by peer reaction, just as comprehension of information will be.

Sensitivity to the importance of including disabled youth in activities with their non-disabled peers is crucial in the area of sexual learning. Not only can young people learn together about themselves as sexual beings, but also non-disabled adolescents can utilize such opportunities to explore and confront common myths about the disabilities of their peers. In classes or programs having sexual learning as a common ground, additional learning may occur spontaneously as students mingle, discuss, interact, and debate issues of importance in their lives. Certainly there are mutual benefits to all adolescents of involving disabled youth in school and community activities that build on shared interests and promote social interaction. In recreational activities, where sexual learning occurs more incidentally, disabled youth will find their self-esteem enhanced by being accepted into existing peer groups and at the same time will benefit from a broad exposure to the many environments in which sexual learning occurs: youth groups, religious organizations, schools, recreational facilities, and community agencies.

Educational Barriers

Educational barriers for disabled youth are quite similar to those for non-disabled young people. School administrators who fear parental objections are reluctant to initiate or to support sex education programs in their schools; teachers are often not knowledgeable or comfortable when they are asked to move beyond anatomical details to broader concepts of sexual learning; and some parents are threatened by the notion that the schools are encroaching on the parental function of sex education, inadequate as many parents may feel about performing this task. Clearly, different tactics must be used to confront the various educational barriers. Chapter Seven offers some strategic suggestions on mobilizing school-community support, emphasizing the importance of a cooperative effort between parents, community professionals, and teachers at curriculum development and instructional techniques.

The Joint Commission on Mental Health of Children (1970) offers compelling reasons for such cooperative efforts:

"To a considerable extent, a child's developing sexuality is associated with his developing emancipation from his family. If he is to grow into an emotionally and sexually mature adult, able to fuse sexual and psychological love in a man-woman relationship, he needs to separate both his sexual self and his psychological self from his parents. Thus, it appears that schools, religious organizations, and other child-serving agencies should share with parents the education of youngsters in matters relating to sex as well as other aspects of the child's developing self."

Cooperation with parents of disabled children, as with all parents, should involve opportunities for the parents to become more comfortable in their roles as sex educators. This may involve parent group discussions about their children's sexual learning needs, parent education groups to increase knowledge and competence as providers of sex information, and advisory group participation to enable parents to take an active role in developing support and designing curriculum materials to promote sexual learning for disabled students.

In some cases, teachers feel a special challenge to meet the needs of disabled students who have been mainstreamed into their classes. Teaching about human sexuality to students with disabilities requires no more and no less special consideration than teaching other content areas. The success in teaching about human sexuality depends greatly on the extent to which the teacher can individualize for students having special needs. In many respects, the best methods for teaching about sexuality to all students are especially well suited to teaching students with special needs:

1. PACING IS IMPORTANT FOR ALL STUDENTS AND MAY HAVE SPECIAL RELEVANCE FOR THE DISABLED STUDENT. A retarded student may need to hear a concept repeated or illustrated in a variety of different ways before it is learned. An emotionally disturbed student may find some material on sexuality threatening or frightening and may communicate the need not to be an involved participant at all times. Students with visual or hearing impairments may receive certain information through the senses but may need other exposure to the same information during the course before being able to integrate it totally into a mean-

ingful frame of reference.

In terms of pacing, the Scarborough teaching method has particular relevance.* Designed originally for use in classes of mentally retarded students, this approach has logical application value for all students. Figure Three illustrates the simple mechanics of the Scarborough: to begin the program with specific and basic concepts and then move outward as far as the individual is capable.

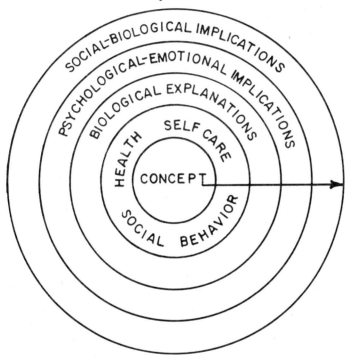

Figure 3. Diagram of Scarborough's Teaching Method.

Since many non-disabled students are already familiar with basic concepts and their applications in health, self-care, and social behavior, these are often taken for granted by the teacher eager to move past the practical issues to values, philosophical issues, and ethical concerns. By keeping in mind the diagram of Scarborough's teaching method, the teacher will be certain to ascertain *each* student's level of concept

*This concept was described by Mrs. Willie Scarborough of the Chicago Public Schools at the Institute on "Retardation and Sexuality," December 3 and 4, 1971 in Philadelphia, Pennsylvania.

comprehension so that individualized instruction, peer support, repeated examples, or additional teaching materials can be used to encourage ongoing learning and integration of new information by the student with special needs.

2. MODELS AND CONCRETE OBJECTS ARE ESPECIALLY GOOD TEACHING TOOLS IN COURSES ABOUT HUMAN SEXUALITY. Models may be used to illustrate size, shape, weight, hardness, surface qualities, temperature, etc. The feel of an anatomical model to a visually impaired student (it is important to clarify whether the model or product is accurate in size and scale); the opportunity for a retarded student to examine a concrete object in minute detail (perhaps with a helpful classmate who can review its function or use); the reinforcement that a hearing-impaired student gains by the visual cues of an object; and the importance for all students of having actual examples to lend reality to the discussion are valid reasons for the teacher to utilize models and concrete objects as supplements to lecture and discussion. In a way, models and concrete objects may be especially appropriate in a human sexuality course, because many students have been denied access or sheltered from learning about body parts or contraception. These and other subjects are ones about which sexually maturing individuals deserve to become fully informed.

3. THE USE OF ROLE PLAYING IS AN IDEAL WAY TO PROMOTE THE INTEGRATION OF FACTS WITH VALUES AND ATTITUDES. The student with special emotional needs will benefit from the reinforcement of reality and the awareness that role played behaviors may serve as guides for more appropriate interaction; the student with a hearing impairment will benefit (as long as the role players face the class) from the situational cues and gestures and body language that accompany the spoken communication; the student who is visually impaired will appreciate vocal inflections and the verbal skills being rehearsed; and the student who is mentally retarded will be able to relate to the role play both as a concrete behavioral example and perhaps to generalize the behaviors to a broader range of appropriate life situations.

4. THE USE OF MOVIES OR FILMSTRIPS PROVIDES BENEFITS SIMILAR TO ROLE PLAYS, ALTHOUGH THE ACTORS AND ACTRESSES ARE ON THE SCREEN RATHER THAN FROM THE CLASSROOM. The role modelings on the screen provide stimuli at different levels for all students, includ-

ing those with disabilities. The important learning from both movies and role plays comes in the group discussion afterwards. At this time the teacher should be alert to encourage the contributions of all students, gearing questions to the messages the acting may have communicated to each.

5. THE USE OF QUESTION-AND-ANSWER SESSIONS PROVIDES AN IDEAL OPPORTUNITY FOR THE TEACHER TO DETECT GAPS IN KNOWLEDGE, TO CORRECT MISINFORMATION, AND TO ADDRESS CONCERNS THAT MAY NOT HAVE BEEN EXPRESSED DURING CLASS DISCUSSIONS. An atmosphere should be created in which *any* question may be asked and no student will be ridiculed, no matter what the question. Often adolescents are silently relieved to realize that they are not the only ones to be unknowledgeable about sexuality; once they cease to be worried about exposing their ignorance, adolescents with a wide range of capabilities can participate openly in the quest for further information.

Teachers can offer a great deal of encouragement to parents who doubt or question their abilities to help their children with sexual learning. As with any other subject, the teacher will want to inform the parent fully of the content to be taught, to inquire about the student's current knowledge and, *most importantly,* to plan for parents to discuss and reinforce in the home what is being taught in the classroom. Although this is a highly desirable goal for parents of all students, it is particularly imporant for parents of those students whose disabilities may prevent them from readily comprehending the material presented in a course where sexuality is discussed.

Reich and Harshman (1971) maintain that the goal of sex education for youth with disabilities must be the same as for all individuals (i.e. to develop young people who are not only sexually fulfilled persons but who also understand themselves, their behaviors and their value systems). This is a tremendous challenge to the community, where no one resource is enough by itself to overcome existing attitudinal, social, and educational barriers. The community that is truly committed to improving the sexual learning of disabled youth must mobilize a broad range of resources. Such resources, in the long run, undoubtedly will enhance the sexual learning of non-disabled youth as concerned community members realize that the key focus need not be on disabilities but, rather, on promoting community involvement toward quality sexual learning.

REFERENCES

Gordon, S. Missing in special education: sex. *The Journal of Special Education,* 5:351-354, 1971.

Joint Commission on Mental Health of Children. *Crisis in Child Mental Health: Challenge for the 1970s.* New York: Harper and Row, 1970.

Kempton, W. Sex education — a cooperative effort of parent and teacher. *Exceptional Children, 41*:531-535, 1975.

Kempton, W. *Sex Education for Persons with Disabilities that Hinder Learning: A Teacher's Guide.* North Scituate, Massachusetts: Duxbury Press, 1975.

Maddock, J. Sex education for the exceptional person: a rationale. *Exceptional Children, 40:*273-278, 1974.

Reich, M.L., and Harshman, H. Sex education for handicapped children: reality or repression? *The Journal of Special Education, 5:*373-377, 1971.

Resource Materials

American Foundation for the Blind. *Sex Education for the Visually Handicapped in Schools and Agencies.* New York: American Foundation for the Blind, 1975.

Ballou, M. et al. *Sex Education and Family Life Curriculum.* Watertown, Massachusetts: Perkins School for the Blind, 1977.

Bass, M.S., and Gelof, M. (Eds.). *Sexual Rights and Responsibilities of the Mentally Retarded,* rev. ed., 1975. Available from M. S. Bass, 216 Glenn Rd., Ardmore, Pennsylvania.

Bass, S. *Sex Education for the Handicapped.* Eugene, Oregon: E.C. Brown Center for Family Studies.

Blacklidge, V. *Sex Education for the Mentally Retarded.* San Leandro, California: Mental Retardation Service, 1968.

Carolina Population Center. *Organizing Community Resources in Sexuality Counseling and Family Planning for the Retarded.* Chapel Hill, North Carolina: Carolina Population Center, University of North Carolina.

Cooksey, P., and Brown, P. *Guide for Teaching Human Sexuality to the Mentally Handicapped.* St. Paul, Minnesota: Planned Parenthood of Minnesota, Inc., 1977.

Council for Exceptional Children. *Sex Education: A Selective Bibliography.* Reston, Virginia: Council for Exceptional Children.

de la Cruz, F., and La Veck, G. *Human Sexuality and the Mentally Retarded.* New York: Brunner/Mazel, 1973.

Dickman, I. *Sex Education and Family Life for Visually Handicapped Children and Youth: A Resource Guide.* New York: American Foundation for the Blind, Inc., and SIECUS, 1975.

Frischer, H.L., Krajicek, M.J., and Borthick, W.A. *Teaching Concepts of Sexual Development to the Developmentally Disabled: A Guide for Parents, Teachers, and Professionals.* Denver: J.F.K. Child Development Center, University of Colorado, 1973.

Gordon, S. *On Being the Parent of a Handicapped Youth: A Guide to Enhance the*

Self-Image of Physically and Learning Disabled Adolescents and Young Adults. Syracuse, New York: Center of Concern, 1975.

Gordon, S. *Sex Education for Neglected Youth: Retarded, Handicapped, Emotionally Disturbed and Learning Disabled.* Syracuse, New York: Institute for Family Research and Education, 1973.

Gordon, S. *Sexual Rights for the People . . . Who Happen to be Handicapped.* Charlottesville, Virginia: Ed-U-Press, 1975.

Gordon, S., Welning, C., Kratovill, B.L., and Biklen, D. *Living Fully: A Guide for Young People with a Handicap, Their Parents, Their Teachers, and Professionals.* Charlottesville, Virginia: Ed-U-Press, 1975.

Heslinga, K. *Not Made of Stone – The Sexual Problems of Handicapped People.* Springfield, Illinois: Charles C Thomas, 1974.

Hopper, C.E., and Allen, W.A. *Sex Education for Physically Handicapped Youth. Springfield, Illinois: Charles C Thomas, 1980.*

Johnson, W.R. *Sex Education and Counseling of Special Groups: The Mentally and Physically Handicapped, Ill, and Elderly.* Springfield, Illinois: Charles C Thomas, 1975.

Kempton, W. *Guidelines for Planning a Training Course on the Subject of Human Sexuality and the Retarded.* Philadelphia: Planned Parenthood of Southeastern Pennsylvania, 1973.

Kempton, W. *Sex Education for Persons with Disabilities that Hinder Learning: A Teacher's Guide.* North Scituate, Massachusetts: Duxbury Press, 1975.

Kempton, W. *A Teacher's Guide to Sex Education for Persons with Learning Dis-'abilities.* North Scituate, Massachusetts: Duxbury Press, 1975.

Kempton, W., Bass, M., and Gordon, S. *Love, Sex and Birth Control for the Mentally Retarded: A Guide for Parents.* Philadelphia: Planned Parenthood of Southeastern Pennsylvania, 1971.

Kempton, W., and Forman, R. *Guidelines for Training in Sexuality and the Mentally Handicapped.* Philadelphia: Planned Parenthood of Southeastern Pennsylvania, 1976.

Kimberly-Clark Corporation. *Growing Up Young: About Menstruation for Parents and Teachers of the Retarded Girl.* Neenah, Wisconsin: Kimberly-Clark Corporation, 1971.

Love, Sex and Birth Control for the Mentally Retarded – A Guide for Parents. Charlottesville, Virginia: Ed-U-Press, 1975. (Also available in Spanish.)

Mooney, T., and Coles, T. *Sexual Options for Paraplegics and Quadriplegics.* Boston: Little, Brown and Co., 1975.

Neff, J. *Sex Education for the Visually Handicapped in Schools and Agencies . . . Selected Papers.* New York: American Foundation for the Blind, 1975.

Planned Parenthood of Minnesota, Inc. *Selected Bibliography on Sexuality, Sex Education and Family Planning for use in Mental Retardation Programs.* Minneapolis, Minnesota: Planned Parenthood of Minnesota, Inc., 1976.

Rolett, K. *Organizing Community Resources in Sexuality Counseling and Family*

35

and Family Planning for the Retarded: A Community Worker's Manual. Chapel Hill, North Carolina: Carolina Population Center, 1976.

Thaller K., and Thaller, B. *Sexuality and the Mentally Retarded.* Washington, D.C.: Office of Economic Opportunity, 1973.

University of California Medical School. *Sexuality and the Cerebral Palsied.* San Francisco: University of California Medical School.

Volpe, E.P. *Human Heredity and Birth Defects.* New York: Bobbs-Merrill Company, Inc., 1971.

The following publications of The Sex Information and Education Council of the United States are available from Behavioral Publications, 72 Fifth Avenue, New York, New York 19911.

A Bibliography of Resources in Sex Education for the Mentally Retarded, 1973.

A Resource Guide in Sex Education for the Mentally Retarded, 1976.

Developing Community Acceptance of Sex Education for the Mentally Retarded, by Medora S. Bass, 1972.

Sex Education and Family Life for Visually Handicapped Children and Youth, 1975.

CHAPTER 4

PEER SUPPORT NETWORKS

Adolescence is a stage of the life cycle during which the peer group assumes an increasingly important function as the adolescent tries out and discards different roles in the search for identity. The peer group can bestow status and approval on the individual, enforce or create social mores (e.g. what to wear, how to act on a date), determine attitudes, and encourage or discourage certain behaviors. Such peer group functions enable the adolescent to achieve the transition from dependence on the family to autonomy. Since peer groups take over some of the parental roles of support and value givers, they are a powerful socializing influence. Rather than undermining parents' relationships with their children, peer groups serve to present alternative values or to encourage adolescents to challenge value systems that may seem outmoded and irrelevant to their lives. Since sexuality and sex are often difficult and awkward topics for parents to discuss with their children, adolescents frequently reach out to their peers for information. Adolescents, influenced by the media, sexually stereotyped adult messages and incomplete factual information, may be a source of mutual misinformation rather than responsive support for their friends.

Numerous community agencies seek to penetrate peer networks in order to bring accurate information and services about sexuality to the attention of adolescents. Social service agencies which have effectively utilized peer communication include Planned Parenthood Associations, government-funded contraceptive clinics, crisis counseling centers, hotlines, drug abuse centers, youth bureaus, and school-based sex education programs.

Since the 1960s the use of youth hotlines has provided an impetus to support the concept of peer counseling. Adolescents rarely view one another with the suspicion and distress they display toward some adults and providers of conventional services. Agencies and educational services have begun to build on the natural communication network existing among peers by training and supporting programs run by peer counselors.

In family planning clinics the training may be focused primarily on issues relating to sexuality and contraception. An example of one such program is that sponsored by the Planned Parenthood Association of Marin County in San Rafael, California. In 1976-77 this program recruited and trained 16 peer counselors in three high schools. The counselors were recruited from classes in human sexuality and trained in six evening sessions that covered empathy, listening skills, and information about sexuality and contraception. Each counselor was then asked to lead teen ''rap'' sessions at the local Planned Parenthood Clinic, under the supervision of an adult teen coordinator. Although no counseling was formally scheduled in the high schools, a great deal of informal counseling and information-giving occurred.

Peer counseling sponsored in school settings is usually designed to incorporate sexuality as only one possible component. An example of a school peer counseling program was developed at George Mason High School in Falls Church, Virginia in 1975. Twenty-four peer counselors were recruited from courses in human relations and sex education and trained by enrolling in two or three peer counseling courses, including a practicum experience. They received school credit for this activity and counseled their peers on a wide range of topics such as study skills, personal adjustment problems, and family relationships, as well as on contraception and sexuality.

A ''near peer'' counseling arrangement exists in the high school in Newark Valley, New York. Here the Tioga County Family Planning Agency has obtained the use of a counseling room, which is staffed once a week by a Cornell University social work student. The student, participating in a 400-hour field placement at Tioga Family Planning receives a lengthy orientation prior to a supervised placement in the high school. This program, which began in 1975, permits adolescents to share their concerns on sexuality, relationships, self-esteem, and contraception with a college student only a few years older than they are. In addition to providing a positive role model for students who come to the counseling room, the Cornell student offers both individual and group counseling, thereby infusing the peer communication network with accurate information and creating a forum for the adolescents to discuss a variety of issues of common concern.

In 1979 the County Youth Bureau in Cortland, New York offered training sessions for peer counselors who attended the local high school. Evening sessions and a weekend retreat provided opportunities for the adolescents to learn counseling skills, community resources, and out-reach interventions. Problems relating to sexuality were discussed, along with other problems experienced by adolescents in the Cortland community: loneliness, low self-esteem, family and peer relationships, and school achievement. The peer counselors hold regular meetings as a group during the school year when they are offering friendship, counseling, and support services to their high school acquaintances.

Members of peer support networks are variously identified as peer counselors, peer advisors, peer communicators, and peer educators. Although the choice of designation in part is determined by the function of the peer support network, some groups are concerned that counseling connotes therapy and advising connotes giving advice, neither of which is an appropriate role in peer support. If the term, *peer counseling* or *peer advising,* is selected, it is important to stress that the main function of the peer counselor/advisor is to be a nonjudgmental and interested listener who can help a troubled peer to explore feelings and options and who can suggest school or community resources that are appropriate sources of ongoing help.

Identification of potential peer counselors can be accomplished in several ways. However, it is important to keep in mind that peer counselors ideally should represent many strata of the student population, including grade levels, racial and ethnic groups, social cliques, and extracurricular interest areas. Therefore, choosing peer counselors who seem to be the "leaders" of the school (from among student council representatives or honor society members) may in fact result in a very homogeneous group of academic achievers or socially popular individuals, leaving unrepresented large groups of students who are less visible in terms of student activities or achievements.

Whatever selection method is chosen, students should be involved at the very earliest stages, whether in making announcements in homeroom, writing articles for the school newspaper, designing posters, or assessing the representativeness of the individuals who indicate an interest. These early involvements will enhance the esprit de corps of the peer counselors and will help them to feel a genuine investment in the ongoing efforts of the peer support network.

In order to achieve heterogeneity in the peer counseling group, articles in the school newspaper can serve as effective recruitment mechanisms, supplemented by posters in the hallways asking interested students to come to an initial meeting where more information will be available. A second technique might be to select an advisory committee or steering committee of six or eight interested students and have them nominate others whom they believe to possess the qualities needed in a peer counselor. Invitations could then be extended by members of the steering committee to the selected individuals, taking care to achieve the balance so necessary to an effective peer counseling network.

Having faculty members identify potential peer counselors has both advantages and disadvantages. Faculty members are probably able to identify students who take their work seriously and who perform their academic duties conscientiously, but they should not assume that responsible classroom behavior correlates with respect and influence generated among peers. Also, faculty are accustomed to seeing students in classroom groupings and may be less aware of the social ties that exist outside of the classroom and even outside of the school environment. For these reasons, even if faculty identify and recruit potential peer counselors, student opinion should be solicited regarding the representativeness of the recruits.

The initial meeting of interested students should provide high visibility of students already involved in the recruitment effort. The faculty sponsor(s) should be present, but should share with the steering committee the responsibility for acquainting interested students with the concept of peer counseling. In the meeting, an effort should be made to present both information and some affective components relating to peer counseling.

An agenda might include:
1. Statement of importance of peer support networks
2. Why "friendship" is not always enough
   a. friends often try to give advice
   b. friends may not know of helpful school and community resources
   c. some people feel they have no friends
   d. some friends betray information shared in confidence

3. What peer counseling offers beyond friendship
   a. an open-minded listener
   b. someone who helps a troubled person to explore his/her feelings, but who does not give advice
   c. appropriate referrals to school and community resources
   d. confidentiality
   e. a willingness to reach out to others who seem lonely and without friends
4. A role play illustrating how a peer counselor might respond to a troubled peer
5. Statement of expectations for persons who enter peer counseling training
   a. time commitment for training and ongoing counseling efforts
   b. confidentiality
   c. willingness to reach out to others

Two concerns that must be anticipated in peer counseling groups are confidentiality and dropouts. Barbara B. Varenhorst (1978) provides some guidelines on the use of confidentiality by peer counselors:

1. Personal information learned from friends should not be shared with others, unless the peer counselor is given permission by the counselee to do so.
2. If a peer counselor cannot be trusted to keep confidence he/she cannot be an effective counselor.
3. In talking about the peer counselor training sessions, the peer counselors may wish to share their excitement and enthusiasm with family or friends. Sharing activities and skills is permissible; sharing content, examples and group confidences is not.
4. In order to be effective in counseling other students, a peer counselor may feel the need to discuss a specific problem before continuing further counseling with a counselee. Preferably the problem should be discussed with the peer counseling leader without mentioning the name of the counselee. If the identity of the counselee must be divulged, the counselee should be asked for permission to reveal it.
5. If, for the protection of the counselee, it is not possible to obtain permission in advance to discuss his/her identity and problem

situation, the counselee should be informed as soon as possible of actions taken by the peer counselor.

6. Any peer counselor who is found to have broken the trust of confidentiality should be dropped from the peer counseling program.

Periodically, either during the training sessions or in active counseling work, a peer counselor may decide to leave the program. Indeed, some peer counseling programs have found the dropout rate to be a major block to continuing or strengthening the peer counseling program. Dropouts should be anticipated when doing initial recruitment, so that a somewhat larger group can be trained than is ultimately desired.

In order to convey a message of the importance of the program to peer counselors, the peer counseling leader must be realistic in terms of allotting sufficient time to the program. Ideally, more than one person will serve as group leader, to provide for variety in role models as well as some encouragement and energy replenishment when demands of the program are great. Additional leaders or several consultants available to the primary leader can also be helpful as recruitment, training, and program development efforts are maintained.

Adolescents who choose to leave the program should not be made to feel guilty about this choice. Perhaps unanticipated time commitments have occurred; perhaps personal problems prevent them from feeling they can help others with their difficulties; perhaps the initial anticipation and enthusiasm fall short as the realities of peer counseling become more apparent. Whenever possible, a student discontinuing the program should have a concluding interview with the peer counseling leader. Programmatically it is important to keep track of reasons that students leave the program; additionally, it may provide an ideal opportunity to help a student think through the decision and to feel comfortable with it.

Too often, teens do not seek help from conventional social service agencies until they are in crisis, or until they suspect a crisis, such as an unwanted pregnancy or venereal disease. Thus, true preventive work often relies on those peer-related services that do exist. By providing information which can guide an adolescent in making responsible decisions, or by providing an appropriate referral to a teen needing specialized counseling or services, peer counselors can be the first critical link in an existing network of community services. Peer counselors are a promising resource in promoting accurate sexual learning and en-

42

couraging the appropriate use of community services.

Although the content of any peer couseling training sessions will depend greatly on the training goals, most trainers will want to include material on basic counseling skills and information on services available to adolescents in the community. Since each community's services and resources are unique, knowledgeable agency staff members may be useful as panel members or facilitators when conveying specific information. Most of the counseling skills taught in peer counseling programs emphasize communications skills, empathy, and active listening. Examples of such skills included in a manual by Allen Ivey and Norma Gluckstern (1974) are:

1. MAINTAINING EYE CONTACT. This does not mean a piercing stare, but rather a sharing of eye contact between two persons that conveys nonverbally the peer counselor's interest and concern.

2. BODY LANGUAGE. The posture of leaning slightly forward often communicates to the counselee that the counselor is alert to what is being communicated. Other body language such as frowns, wrinkles of the brow, smiles, tapping fingers, clenching fists, and surprised looks all convey messages without words. Peer counselors will need to be sensitive to the messages their body language might convey in a helping relationship.

3. MINIMAL ENCOURAGERS. The purpose of minimal encouragers is to assist and support the counselee in sharing problems and concerns. Examples include: "Mmm hmm," "tell me more," "then?" "and?" or the repetition of one or two key words. Silence can also serve as a minimal encourager if it is perceived by the counselee as an opportunity to sort out thoughts, to articulate ideas, and to feel accepted by the peer counselor.

4. SILENCE. One skill which is frequently misunderstood or ignored by peer counselors is silence. Young people often believe that talking is the best indication that help is being offered. Thus, they strive for a constant stream of conversation, feeling a sense of anxiety when silence occurs. This results in silences being hastily filled, often ignoring the pacing needs that the counselee may have. Once peer counselors can appreciate that silence has many positive functions, they can be encouraged to utilize silences constructively in their interactions:

— Silence can provide an opportunity for the troubled person to

43

reflect on ideas that have been raised in discussion.

— Silence can provide an opportunity for peers to shape or to weigh in their minds the issues they want to pursue as the conversation continues.

— Silence can communicate a tacit sense of respect for the other's need to influence the pacing of the conversation.

— A comfortable silence can promote a sense of mutual camaraderie between young people.

5. OPEN AND CLOSED QUESTIONS. Open questions are those which require a certain amount of detail in order for an adequate answer to be communicated. Open questions might include such phrases as: ''Tell me about . . .''; ''How did you feel about that?''; ''How have things been going?''; ''Could you tell me more about that?''; or ''Could you give me a specific example?'' The advantage of open questions is that they permit the counselee to answer in his/her own words while feeling the interest and support of the counselor.

Closed questions usually require brief, factual answers and do not tap the feeling or emotions of the counselee. A difficulty with closed questions is that the counselor asking such questions may find that he/she is leading the interview, rather than encouraging the counselee to communicate freely about the dimensions of the problem being discussed. A peer counselor who relies heavily on closed questions is often forced to concentrate so hard on thinking up the next question that he/she neglects to attend to what the counselee is communicating. Examples of closed questions and open questions enable us to see these differences more clearly:

Closed Question	*Open Question*
How many brothers and sisters do you have?	Could you tell me about your family?
What is your favorite subject?	How do you feel about your courses this year?
Do you get along with your boyfriend/girlfriend?	How are things going with your boyfriend/girlfriend?

6. THE PARAPHRASE. Paraphrasing can be used to reflect either content or feeling. A paraphrase is a restatement of a communication. The function of the paraphrase is to check out with the counselee the meaning

of his/her perceived message and to share with the counselee one's understanding of his/her communication. A paraphrase is not a verbatim repetition of the counselee's message but, rather, the counselor's restatement of that message in slightly different words.

Paraphrase of Content: Paraphrasing content involves capturing the essence of the *factual* message being communicated. It provides an opportunity to ascertain the accuracy with which the peer counselor has perceived the message. Examples of paraphrases of content might include:

Counselee	*Peer Counselor*
My subjects are all so hard.	You are having a tough time with your courses.
My parents are completely unpredictable.	You don't always know what to expect from your parents.
Nobody likes me.	You don't believe that you have any friends.

Paraphrase of Feeling: Paraphrasing feeling is a method of reaching for the emotions which are either stated verbally, or implied nonverbally. In order to paraphrase the feeling in a statement, the counselor must first identify the emotion behind the message.

Counselee	*Peer Counselor*
My boyfriend flirts too much.	You're irritated by your boyfriend's flirting.
School is such a bore.	School really turns you off.
I can't wait for vacation!	You're really excited at getting some time off.

There is always the possibility that a peer counselor will misinterpret or misunderstand the feeling being communicated. However, in such cases the counselee is likely to offer more accurate input, as the following examples show:

Counselee	*Peer Counselor*
My sister is going away to college next week.	So you're sad to see her go?
Oh no — I'm happy, because	

45

now I can have our room to
myself!
I got a B + in math.   You must be pleased to have
done so well.
Actually I'm kind of disappointed;
I was hoping for an A.

The use of active listening skills by the peer counselor enables the counselee to share his/her concerns fully. In some cases the mere sharing and exploring of those concerns may be sufficient to relieve anxiety, guilt, or loneliness. However, it is critical that counselors be able to provide information and referral services to their peers if a problem requires more specialized or clinical intervention. Because of the eagerness of peer counselors to be helpful in all situations, it is especially important for training to stress that the most appropriate form of help may involve referral and follow up in order to be certain that the troubled individual is getting more specialized help than the peer counselor is equipped to offer. In the referral process, the peer counselor can be a critical link by offering information about an appropriate community service and perhaps by accompanying a peer as he/she makes application for services.

REFERENCES

Ivey, A., and Gluckstern, N. *Basic Attending Skills: Participant Manual.* North Amherst, Massachusetts: Microtraining Associates, Inc., 1974.

Varenhorst, B. *Curriculum Guide for Student Peer Counseling Training.* Palo Alto, California: Palo Alto Unified School District, 1978.

Resource Materials

Bolton, R. *Communication Skills for Personal and Professional Effectiveness.* Cazenovia, New York: Ridge Consultants, 1975.

Bower, S., and Bower, G. *Asserting Yourself.* Reading, Massachusetts: Addison-Wesley, 1976.

Brammer, M. *The Helping Relationship.* Englewood Cliffs, New Jersey: Prentice-Hall, Inc., 1973.

Gazda, G.M. *Human Relations Development: A Manual for Educators.* Boston: Allyn and Bacon, Inc., 1973.

Gelatt, H.B., Varenhorst, B., Carey, R. and Miller, G. *Decision and Outcomes.* New York: College Entrance Examination Board, 1973.

Hebeisen, A. *Peer Program for Youth.* Minneapolis, Minnesota: Augsburg Publishing House, 1973.

Hamburg, B., and Varenhorst, B. Peer counseling in the secondary schools: a community mental health project for youth. *American Journal of Orthopsychiatry, 42*:566-581, 1972.

Ivey, A., and Gluckstern, N. *Basic Attending Skills: Participant Manual,* North Amherst, Massachusetts: Microtraining Associates, Inc., 1974.

Ivey, A. *Microcounseling: Innovations in Interviewing Training.* Springfield, Illinois: Charles C Thomas, 1971

Johnson, D.E. *Reaching Out.* Englewood Cliffs, New Jersey: Prentice-Hall, Inc., 1972.

Samuels, M., and Samuels, D. *The Complete Handbook of Peer Counseling.* Miami, Florida: Fiesta Publishing Corporation, 1975.

Varenhorst, B. *Curriculum Guide for Student Peer Counseling Training.* Palo Alto, California: Palo Alto Unified School District, 1978.

Varenhorst, B. Hello me . . . hello you: peer counseling interventions. In Mitchel, A., and Johnson, C. (Eds.): *Therapeutic Techniques: Working Models for the Helping Professional.* Fullerton, California: California Personnel and Guidance Association, 1973.

Varenhorst, B. Training adolescents as peer counselors. *Personnel and Guidance. 53:*271-275, 1974.

Varenhorst, B. Peer counseling: a guidance program and a behavioral intervention. In Krumboltz and Thoresen (Eds.): *Counseling Methods.* New York: Holt, Rinehart and Winston, 1976.

CHAPTER 5

PARENTS AS SEX EDUCATORS OF THEIR CHILDREN

Parents face a difficult challenge as their children become adolescents. Not only must they help their children through the normal turmoil of the teen years, but they must also complete developmental tasks of their own. What are some of the challenges faced by parents of adolescents?

Sexuality

At the very time the adolescent is maturing sexually, the parent must face certain aspects of his/her own sexuality that have been dormant. Change in sexual vigor and real or anticipated concerns about menopause are issues for parents at a time that their adolescents' own burgeoning sexuality reminds them of the freshness, vitality, and youth that is now in their past. Menopause may potentially have a positive and invigorating effect on the parents' sexual relationship, permitting an enjoyment of sexual pleasure without the accompanying fear of pregnancy. Some parents respond to the highly charged sexual atmosphere of the home by withdrawing from one another; others may decide to have "one last fling" while they are still considered desirable sexual partners. Either of these choices results in strains in the marriage which, in turn, will diminish the amount of energy that parents have to devote to the needs of their adolescent. Parents, too, are often envious of the greater sexual freedom that adolescents have today and may feel regrets at not having experienced such freedom during their teenage years prior to marriage. This envy may make it especially difficult for the parent to set consistent behavioral limits for the adolescent and, in some cases, contributes to the parent's getting vicarious pleasure from the child's sexual adventures. In single parent families where the parent is dating, the issue of parental sexuality is one that the adolescent must confront. There may be feelings of competitiveness or rivalry between the parent

48

and the adolescent as both strive to be sexually attractive, socially at ease, and respected in a caring relationship. Single parents may be uncertain how much of their own sexual behavior should be discreet or whether they dare impose values upon the adolescent that they are not observing in their own sexual relations.

The most secure framework within which an adolescent can experiment with new behaviors and arrive at a sense of values is in a household where both parents have come to terms with the changes in their sexuality and do not need to use the adolescent either to avoid or to stimulate their own feelings about sexuality. Parents need to communicate pride to their teenagers about their efforts to grow and mature, yet to set limits and to share the values that are important to them.

Loss of Control

Parents, for whom parenthood has meant guiding and protecting their children, face resentful and rebellious behavior by the adolescent if too much control is exercised over his/her behavior. Parents who had a difficult adolescence (or whose parents did not provide helpful role models for the current challenge) feel especially ambivalent about how much control to wield and how much to leave to the adolescent's discretion. It is hard for parents to allow their adolescents to make mistakes, yet adolescents often learn best by experiencing for themselves rather than believing a parental edict. Parents, too, have their egos wrapped up in their children and if they fear that their teenager might bring disgrace, shame or embarrassment to the family, they may feel compelled to exercise greater control. Parents need to see themselves as ''good parents'' and any threat to that role satisfaction may be responded to without sufficient attention to the adolescent's need for increasing independence in decision making.

Rebellion and limit testing are natural and expected aspects of an adolescent's responses to parental limits. The parents must then decide which limits are the important ones on which to exercise firmness and which limits permit room for parent-child negotiation and subsequent adolescent experimentation.

49

Parenting Roles

At the time that their child is reaching adolescence, parents have been in the parental role for a number of years and often feel the need for a respite at the very time that the adolescent will need special help with developmental turmoils. Because of the adolescent's increasing maturity, parents are often able to reinvest in old hobbies, to have a more active social life, to take some vacations without the children, to experiment with new or expanded career choices, and generally to expand their roles beyond that of parent. It is at this time of the parent's life cycle, however, that their own parents may become increasingly needy and dependent as they face diminishing physical energy, declining health, shrinking financial reserves, and often unmet emotional needs for which they seek support. The role reversal in which the adult child becomes a nurturing and supportive resource for the dependent parent can present resentments. The adult child begins to feel as though he is depleted of energy and has fewer resources available for meeting his own emotional needs. If the grandparent is demanding, critical, or intrusive, the parent may be pulled between seeking approval and needing some autonomy from incessant demands. Marital tensions can occur as one spouse may need to divide time, attention, and financial resources between the family and the elderly parents. Guilt about not being able to do enough for one's elders comes at a time when the adolescent is loudly protesting that parents are trying to control his/her life too much! This is a stage of life that often leaves parents feeling depleted, often without sufficient resources to replenish their physical and emotional reserves of energy.

Personal Achievement

The theme of achievement is a varied one in families with adolescents. Parents may be at the peaks of their careers or, conversely, at a point where they must come to terms with diminishing aspirations or vanished dreams. Sometimes frustrated parental hopes of achievement are displaced onto the adolescent, with parents urging their offspring to get ahead, do better, and try harder at the very time that the adolescent wants to channel energies into social as well as vocational or academic pursuits. At the very time when parents may want their child to begin to follow in their footsteps, the adolescent is intent on finding a separate

50

identity and resists being expected to fulfill parental aspirations.

Mothers have a complex vested interest in family achievement patterns. If the mother gains her identity from her homemaking and child-rearing tasks, then she is likely to feel a special sense of loss as the adolescent no longer needs her help and support in old and familiar ways. As the adolescent is striving for independence, the mother's need to be valued may cause her to restrict independence or to communicate messages of doubt about the adolescent's capabilities. If the mother has a career outside of the home, she is less likely to feel unappreciated as her adolescent spends less and less time at home and becomes increasingly absorbed in peer activities and social relationships.

Parents frequently communicate the hope that their children can be more successful than the parents have been. Frequently such hopes clash with the adolescent's ambivalence over whether to strive for parental approval or to try new directions. Sometimes the rejection of parental values is an honest effort by the adolescent to come to terms with his or her own sense of right and wrong; at other times it may be an effort to avoid fears of failure or fears of the demands that ''success'' may impose. In any case, parents are often profoundly disappointed when their child seems to reject the hopes and plans they had nourished for the future. Part of parental achievement is in seeing one's offspring leading a productive and satisfying life; in basking in the reflected glory of a child who is successful in his/her efforts; in feeling that one has helped one's child to get a good start in life. When adolescent behavior and aspirations clash with parental hopes and expectations, parents must deal with their feelings of inadequacy and sometimes of failure, at a time when the young adult will not be bound by parental exhortations to ''get ahead'' or ''do what's good for you.''

Separation

The theme of separation is a continuing one throughout the adolescent years. Parents who, on the one hand, are eager to see their child become self-sufficient and independent, on the other hand, fear the loss to them that young adulthood will bring as the child forms new emotional attachments which are seen as replacing, rather than supplementing, parental love and affection. They are no longer central in the cast of

51

characters in their adolescent's life; the loss of control this represents, along with the diminishing satisfactions in career and homemaking roles, can leave parents feeling sorrowful and empty at the very time the adolescent is bursting with hopes and energy for the future.

Mourning is a natural response to separation, whether actual or impending. Parents and siblings can be expected to feel sorrow, anger, loss, and abandonment as the adolescent moves away from the family constellation, experimenting with the new roles of young adulthood. The adolescent, too, feels emotions related to mourning; in part this accounts for wide mood swings and for feelings of ambivalence about achieving independence. It is not unusual for families to feel a sense of family disintegration at the prospect of the adolescent's independence. Frances Scherz (1967) points out that "the crisis of separation and mourning is transitory, however, and eventually a 'new' family will arise — one in which the adolescent will have become an independent adult, connected by affectional ties to parents who have grown closer to each other."

However, in some families, parents have great difficulty developing a new and closer relationship once the adolescent is grown. For parents who have stayed together for the sake of the children, for parents whose investment in parenting roles enabled them to deny or avoid marital incompatibilities, or for parents who have utilized the adolescent as a companion and a confidante in place of a spouse, the anticipation of separation may exacerbate existing martial tensions. Some parents respond by trying desperately to bind the adolescent to the family, thereby denying his/her need to separate and often undermining the adolescent's self-esteem when he/she attempts to achieve independence. Often parents provoke feelings of guilt in the adolescent so that autonomy is equated with inattentiveness or insensitivity to family needs. Indeed, the very real marital discord that may erupt between parents as their adolescent searches for an identity beyond the family can be convincing evidence for parents as they seek to communicate their continuing need for the adolescent to keep the peace in the family. Sonya Rhodes (1977) points out that if the family system is one in which belonging is achieved at the expense of difference, the family may overprotect and invade the older adolescent's life in a way that binds him or her to the family even further. In these families, compliance and conformity become the keys to parental approval, and adolescent attempts at learning new life skills are rejected or are subverted to serve the family's interests and to perpetuate its solidarity.

Some parents, in their efforts to avoid perceiving and working through their feelings of loss and separation, may force the adolescent to disengage prematurely from the family. This may occur at a time when the adolescent is testing limits by asking for more independence than he/she really wants or it may occur in anger when parents feel they can no longer tolerate the tension and antagonism the adolescent causes in the home. In either case, if the adolescent leaves home at the behest of the parents, rather than as an outgrowth of personal maturity, all family members are left with unresolved feelings about the separation.

Rhodes (1977) believes that what is significant in those families that bind or expel disengaging members is the parents' total inability to tolerate experimentation or difference. The adolescent's developmental task of achieving a separate identity is bound to challenge the parents' capacity for tolerance and flexibility; to the extent that parents can respond with resilience and a willingness to renegotiate the boundaries of the parent-child relationship, the family can reorganize without denying the adolescent the opportunity to experiment and strive for increasing autonomy. How, then, are parental attitudes affected by the developmental tasks that they face? First, we must acknowledge that parents are raising their children at a time when the values that made sense twenty to thirty years ago will probably be viewed by today's adolescents as outmoded, irrelevant, or old fashioned. This is particularly true in the area of sexuality. Although the fear of pregnancy remains a powerful deterrent to many, the availability of birth control and abortion seems to offer alternatives to pregnancy for some sexually active adolescents.

Only by appreciating the unique life cycle challenges faced by parents is it possible to design programs which respond first to *adult* developmental tasks and second to parents' needs to become more comfortable and informed sex educators of their children. Despite assertions by parents that they should be viewed as the primary sex educators of their children, the home is not the environment in which youth gain extensive sexual learning. Study after study reveal that parents, especially fathers, feel awkward talking with their children about sexual issues and, as a result, provide very little information that young people find helpful.

53

In a 1979 study by Ross of 1000 New York City teens, only 25 percent of the respondents indicated that their parents had discussed birth control with them. A 1978 study by Roberts, Kline, and Gagnon of over 1,400 Cleveland parents of children ages three to eleven revealed that few of the parents interviewed had ever discussed any aspect of erotic activity with their children.

A two-year survey in the mid-1960s (Furstenberg, 1976) of pregnant adolescents registering for prenatal care in a Baltimore clinic found that vague contraceptive instruction had almost the same impact on adolescents as no instruction. The same study revealed that, in families where the mother and daughter discussed birth control, 52 percent of the adolescents had had some experience with birth control, compared with 23 percent from families in which no guidance was given. This confirms studies cited by Gordon, Scales, and Everly (1979) which indicate that teenagers who have talked to their parents about sex are likely to delay first intercourse and then to use contraception when they do become sexually active.

A three-year survey of more than 800 college students by Gordon, Scales, and Everly (1979) found that parents were consistently reported as minimally contributing to their children's education about sex. The United States Commission on Obscenity (1970) reported that fathers provided sex education for a mere 10 percent of adults and teenagers. What are the reasons which cause parents, on the one hand, to prefer to be the primary source of sexual information and values for their children and, on the other hand, to be apprehensive about openly discussing sexual issues with their offspring?

Parents learn much about parenting from viewing their own parents as role models. Yet parents were even less likely twenty-five years ago to have talked with their children beyond the "birds and bees." So today's parents have little to draw from in their own backgrounds to guide them in their efforts at increasing their children's sexual learning. Further, their knowledge about human sexuality may have been limited to a brief (probably sex-segregated) session in a health or biology class that focused on anatomy but answered none of the questions that curious young people seek answers to. Issues like venereal disease, homosexuality, and masturbation are not likely to be ones that parents are comfortable with on a factual basis — not to mention the emotional basis!

Many parents fear that providing information about sexuality to adolescents will cause them to become sexually active. What parents must appreciate is that children and adolescents are increasing their sexual learning in many community environments. Repeated studies show that peers and the media are the most utilized sources of information about sex by young people. And yet these very sources are recognized by parents to be unreliable and distorted in their presentation of information. A 1973 study by Lewis found that sex education received from friends "seems to be associated with more permissive sexual behavior."

Adolescents are adept at seeming more knowledgeable than they actually are. Parents who are reluctant to initiate discussions of sexual issues often rationalize that "kids today know so much more than I did at their age." Too, an adolescent may sense a parent's reluctance to talk openly and save them both from mutual discomfort by claiming sufficient knowledge about sexual matters. The earlier a young person has sexual intercourse, the less informed he or she is likely to be; yet, adolescents often exhibit a façade of being sexually knowledgeable to pretend they understand as much as their experience suggests.

A 1979 survey by Ross asked 950 New York City adolescents how much information they thought they had about reproduction and contraception. Fifty-six percent of the respondents felt they knew "enough," yet only 31 percent of that group indicated that they had heard about the eight forms of contraception listed on the questionnaire. In the same New York City study, 882 adolescents were asked when conception was most likely to occur. Only 35 percent of the 480 respondents who felt they knew "enough" about birth control gave the correct response of "halfway between one period and the next." Clearly parents should not accept at face value their adolescents' claims to have sufficent knowledge about human sexuality, reproduction, and contraception.

The next stumbling block to parents seems to be whether they possess adequate information themselves. Some fear that they will be asked a question they cannot answer; others are concerned that they will not have the correct vocabulary for communicating information; still others are apprehensive about harming their offspring by inadvertently providing inaccurate information. First, it is important for parents to realize they know far more than most of their children. For the child who stumps a parent with a question, the best response is, ''I don't know, but let's see if we can find out together.'' The local library, the school nurse, the family doctor, or the encyclopedia are all ready resources that parent and child can consult. Children are often more comfortable in asking questions if they know that their parents will help them identify the available resources for obtaining accurate information. Likewise, if a parent inadvertently communicates inaccurate information to a child, the most sensible response is to correct it at the earliest opportunity. Children can accept errors without losing respect for the parent. The important message for the parent to communicate is that accurate sources do exist when one is in doubt of specific information on any subject.

Many children are far more interested in knowing about their parents' values than in mastering complex factual information. Parents can utilize many opportunities in daily life to communicate their values and to discuss them with their offspring of all ages. Ann Landers's columns, media messages, political legislation, current events and religious teachings provide a wealth of perspectives for parents and children to examine and discuss.

One opportunity for parents to share their concerns and to become more comfortable as potential sex educators is through a parent discussion group. Most adults appreciate that sexuality is not an easy subject to talk about, and few parents are comfortable initiating or responding to their children's concerns on the topic. A discussion group which accepts parental embarrassment and discomfort can work toward constructive ways to utilize new patterns of communication with children about sexuality. Any effort to work with parents must take into consideration their need for accurate knowledge, an exploration of values and attitudes, and helpful communication techniques.

Accurate Knowledge

One should not assume that parents have an accurate knowledge base until this has been demonstrated. An anonymous pretest is the best way to assess the extent to which beliefs need to be corrected or supplemented. A needs assessment is also a useful tool to distribute as a way of enabling parents to rank-order the topics they especially want to discuss. Data from the pretest and the needs assessment will then enable the parent group leader to be responsive to the knowledge deficits and the interests of the group. Hopefully the early focus on what each individual hopes to gain from the group will encourage parents to feel an investment in the group effort and a willingness to talk openly about the challenges they face as sex educators of their children.

Values and Attitudes

Many parents are reluctant to communicate their values on sexual matters to their adolescents. This reluctance stems from several origins. For those parents who are uncomfortable talking about any sexual issues with their children, discussion of values will be equally uncomfortable. Other parents, especially those who are ambivalent about exercising control or restraint over their adolescents' efforts to grow and learn, are reluctant to set limits in areas where sexual behavior is involved. Still other parents, eager to keep the lines of communication open at a time when adolescents criticize parental attitudes as being old-fashioned, are hesitant to state their values on sexual behavior for fear that their children will withdraw from them in disagreement. Withdrawal is far more likely to occur in those parent-child relationships where parents refuse to discuss issues that relate to sexuality. Parents need not be ashamed of their old-fashioned values and, in fact, may be surprised to realize that their adolescents do want to know where the parents stand, even if they choose not to agree or to adopt the same value stance. Parents should, however, specify that if the adolescent chooses to be sexually active despite parental values which discourage this, he or she should be aware of the possible consequences of sexual activity and should use birth control to protect against unwanted pregnancy. Parents might want to discuss with their adolescents the serious consequences of parenthood: interruption of education, low-paying jobs or unemployment, social isolation, dependence on parents or social services, and (in marriages forced by pregnancy) a 50 percent chance of divorce within five years.

Old-fashioned parents are just as good in their parenting roles as parents with more liberal values and attitudes. The imporant issue is to be honest and straightforward in communicating values and attitudes; too often children conclude from parental silence that their parents are unwilling to talk with them about sexuality. Communication is of ultimate importance; parent discussion groups should focus on helping parents to see how their attitudes get in the way of communicating their values to children, rather than on changing the attitudes per se.

Communication Techniques

Parents who have not felt comfortable in talking with their children about sexual concerns will undoubtedly be reassured to know that they are not alone in these feelings. Those parents in the group who have made efforts to help their children with sexual learning will undoubtedly serve as positive role models for more reluctant parents. Role playing can serve as a facilitating effort for practicing communication skills and for identifying issues and concerns for small and large group discussions.

Just as important as responding to children's questions is the skill of initiating conversations about topics concerned with human sexuality. Children who may have received early subtle messages that sex is a forbidden subject will probably be reluctant to initiate discussions or to ask questions relating to sexual concerns. They may even disregard parental efforts to discuss subjects which had previously been avoided. Parents will need support in identifying "teachable moments" that arise in the course of daily life.

The concept of a parent discussion group is vital in those communities where parents maintain that they are the primary sex educators of their children. Indeed, most parents would like to be comfortable in this role, but various studies show that parents feel great uncertainty about helping their children with sexual learning. It is sometimes this uncertainty about sexual learning in general that causes parents to oppose its incorporation into the school curriculum. Therefore, one impetus for beginning a parents' group might be to explore ways that the school can complement the parents' efforts. Once parents are aware of the materials that can be used in the classroom and once they are helped to be more comfortable with their own roles as sex educators, parents may feel more invested in the concept of cooperation with the schools rather than competition.

What are some considerations that are important before beginning a parent group?

1. *Laying the groundwork*

In a parent group this depends on whether the invited participants will be parents of students or whether the parent group leader has persuaded a community professional to offer the group under the sponsorship of a community agency like a family service agency, a religious institutition, or the local Y. In the former case, publicity would probably be sent home with students or distributed through the PTA; if the group is advertised through the broader community, a variety of groups can publicize the effort: Parents without Partners, continuing education classes, cooperative extension, social agencies, religious organizations, and day care centers. The local newspaper may be willing to run an article featuring the need for sex education for children and adolescents. Newspaper announcements and radio spots can publicize the parent discussion group.

In the publicity for any parent group, it is important to include such information as the dates, locations, and times of the group meetings and whether babysitting is available. Charging fees will discourage some people, so every effort should be made to obtain outside funding for whatever costs are involved. The publicity should state clearly that the group is for education, not for therapy. To whatever extent possible, males and fathers should be encouraged to attend.

2. *Logistical considerations*

WHERE: The location should be easily accessible. In some communities this means near public transportation; in others it means near parking facilities.

WHEN: Assuming that the group is offered in the evening, leaders should plan for 1½ or 2-hour sessions, to extend no later than 9:30. If weekend groups are offered, longer hours may be scheduled at the convenience of the participants.

DURATION: Four to six sessions will allow parents to learn new information and acquire new skills without seeming like an extensive commitment of time. For those parents who request them, additional sessions can be scheduled.

WHO: It is useful to consider having two leaders for several reasons: if areas of expertise differ, the leaders will complement one another in knowledge and skills; if one leader is a male and the other a female, then more balanced participation from the group may be encouraged; two leaders can monitor small groups more easily than one and, lastly, leaders can act as a team in evaluating, planning, and pooling their observations about the group. If only one leader works with the group, it may be useful on occasion to bring in outside speakers. The size of the group should be smaller with only one leader, so that participants can receive enough individualized attention for their needs and concerns.

How MANY: If there is one leader for the group, eight to twelve participants will have ample opportunity for interaction, small group activities, and individual questions. A group with two leaders might be expanded to include as many as sixteen, but more than that will probably seem unwieldy if the group displays good attendance and active participation.

3. *Setting the stage*

The first meeting should include:
   a. finding a large and comfortable room with movable chairs and enough space so the participants can break down into small groups;
   b. nametags may provide a helpful way of getting acquainted;
   c. coffee and other refreshments (perhaps to be provided by group members after the first session) help to promote a relaxed and comfortable atmosphere; and
   d. ascertaining that certain materials are available: paper, pencils, a blackboard or newsprint, magic markers, a projector, and a screen.

4. *The first session*

This is especially important, as it provides an opportunity for the group to establish its goals and for individual members to articulate their concerns. Initial introductions might include names, ages of children, what each individual hopes to gain from the group and perhaps the opportunity to share whatever doubts or apprehensions the parents felt in coming to the group. The subsequent use of an attitude survey or a fact sheet

60

serves the double purpose of allowing the leader to "take stock" of where the group's needs lie and to enable each member of the group to prioritize specific concerns that relate to human sexuality.

An excellent book for persons planning a curriculum for parent groups is *Community Sex Education Programs for Parents* by Sol Gordon (Syracuse: The Institute for Family Research and Education), 1977.

In this book are mentioned several concerns or misconceptions that should be discussed as the stage is set for subsequent sessions:

Many parents are concerned that providing their children with information about sexuality may encourage the children to become sexually active. Parents need help in understanding that ignorance, not knowledge, lies at the root of most adolescent pregnancies. Since sex is a major topic of concern and curiosity for adolescents, parents can be certain that their teenagers are seeking information — from peers, from television and movies, from magazines, none of which necessarily communicates accurate facts or values that parents would want their children to emulate. Once parents can accept that their adolescents are learning about sexuality, it becomes more possible for them to accept their roles as providers of information and values.

Parents are also concerned that they may not be able to communicate about sexual topics "the right way." Parents are fearful of making mistakes or appearing foolish or embarrassed as they communicate information about sexuality to their children. Too often these fears inhibit parents from responding to or initiating conversations on issues related to sex. Once parents recognize that they probably know more than their children, the challenge becomes that of achieving comfort in pursuing discussions with their offspring. Parents must also acknowledge that if they are uncertain how to respond to a specific question, it is acceptable to say "I don't know, but perhaps together we can find a book that will answer the question for both of us." Children will appreciate that learning about sexuality can be a lifelong endeavor and that resources do exist that provide additional information as their questions become more complex.

If the first session is devoted to concerns which have thus inhibited parents from communicating openly with their children on sexual is-

61

sues, later sessions can be organized around topics that parents in the group identify as *their* prime concerns.

It is often tempting to provide parents with numerous brochures, pamphlets, and bibliographies relating to sex education. Helpful though these materials may be, it is far more important in initial sessions to help the parents feel that *they* can become the major resource for their children. A few well chosen pamphlets that parents and children can read or discuss together are preferable to an avalanche of materials that may make parents feel inadequate in their knowledge and which may communicate the message to adolescents that reading can substitute for an exchange of ideas or information between parent and child.

REFERENCES

Furstenberg, F.F. *Unplanned Parenthood: The Social Consequences of Teenage childbearing.* New York: The Free Press, 1976.

Gordon, S. *Community Sex Education Programs for Parents.* Syracuse, New York: The Institute for Family Research and Education, 1977.

Gordon, S., Scales, P., and Everly, K. *The Sexual Adolescent.* North Scituate, Massachusetts: Duxbury Press, 1979.

Lewis, R.A. Parents and peers: socialization agents in the coital behavior of young adults. *Journal of Sex Research, 9*:156-170, 1973.

Rhodes, S. A developmental approach to the life cycle of the family. *Social Casework, 58*:301-311, 1977.

Roberts, E., Kline, D., and Gagnon, J. *Family Life and Sexual Learning: A Study of the Role of Parents in the Sexual Learning of Children.* Cambridge, Massachusetts: Population Education, Inc., 1978.

Ross, S. *The Youth Values Project.* Washington, D.C.: The Population Institute, 1979.

Scherz, F. The crisis of adolescence in family life. *Social Casework, 48*:209-215, 1967.

United States Commission on Obscenity and Pornography. *Report of the Commission.* New York: Bantam Books, 1970.

Resource Materials

Block, W. *What Your Child Really Wants to Know about Sex and Why.* Englewood Cliffs, New Jersey: Prentice-Hall, Inc., 1972.

Braaten-Hanson, S., and Nass, N. *Sexuality Education for Parents.* Jefferson, Wisconsin: Dodge-Jefferson Planned Parenthood, 1979.

Brown, T.E. *Concerns of Parents about Sex Education.* New York: Sex Information and Education Council of the United States, 1971.

Child Study Association — Wel-Met, Inc. *What to Tell Your Children about Sex.* New York: Pocket Books, 1974.

Community Sex Education Center. *Sex Education at Home: A Guide for Parents*. Syracuse, New York: Planned Parenthood Center of Syracuse, Inc., 1974.

Del Solar, C. *Parent's Answer Book*. New York: Grosset and Dunlap, 1971.

Driver, H. *Sex Guidance for Your Child*. Madison, Wisconsin: Monona Publications, 1970.

Gadpaille, W.J. *Father's Role in Sex Education of His Son*. Reprint available from Stanley Kruger, Special Programs Director, Bureau of School Systems, United States Office of Education, 400 Maryland Avenue, SW, Washington, D.C. 20202.

Ginott, H.G. *Between Parent and Teenager*. New York: Avon Books, 1979.

Gochros, J.S. *What to Say after You Clear Your Throat*. Kailua, Hawaii: Press Pacifica, 1980.

Gordon, S., and Dickman, I.R. *Sex Education: The Parent's Role*. Charlottesville, Virginia: Ed-U-Press, 1977.

Gordon, S., Scales, P., and Everly, K. *The Sexual Adolescent: Communicating with Teeangers about Sex*. North Scituate, Massachusetts: Duxbury Press, 1979.

How to Talk to Your Teenagers about Something that's not Easy to Talk About. New York: Planned Parenthood Federation of America, Inc., 1976.

Institute for Family Research and Education. *Community Family Life Education Program for Parents: A Training Manual for Organizers*. Charlottesville, Virginia: Ed-U-Press, 1977.

Landers, A. *High School Sex and How to Deal with it – A Guide for Teens and Their Parents*. Chicago: available from P.O. Box 11995, Chicago, Illinois, 60611. Enclose 50¢ and a large self-addressed stamped envelope.

Lyman, M. *Sex Education at Home: A Guide for Parents*. Syracuse, New York: Planned Parenthood Center of Syracuse, 1974.

McBridge, W., and Fleischhauer-Hardt. *Show Me! A Picture Book of Sex for Children and Parents*. New York: St. Martin's Press, 1975.

McCary, J.L. *A Complete Sex Education for Parents, Teenagers and Young Adults*. New York: Van Nostrand Reinhold, 1973.

Pomeroy, W.B. *Sex and the Family*. New York: Delacorte Press, 1974.

Pomeroy, W.B. *Your Child and Sex: A Guide for Parents*. New York: Dell Publishing Co., Inc., 1976.

Reubens, J.R. *Myth-Information: A Sex Education Game for Families and other Formal and Informal Groups*. Saluda, North Carolina: Family Life Publications, Inc., 1978.

Rubin, I., and Calderwood, D. *A Family Guide to Sex*. New York: Signet Books, New American Library, Inc., 1973.

Scanzoni, L. *Sex is a Parent Affair*, Glendale, California: Regal Books, 1973.

Spain, J. *Your Daughter is Having Sex*. Hoboken, New Jersey: Hoboken Family Planning, Inc., 1980.

Uslander A., and Weiss, C. *Dealing with Questions about Sex*. Maple Plain, Minnesota: Learning Handbooks, 1975.

Uslander, A., Weiss, C., and Telman, J. *Sex Education for Today's Child: A Guide for Modern Parents*. New York: Association Press, 1977.

63

What Teens Want to Know but Don't Know How to Ask. New York: Planned Parenthood
Federation of America, Inc., 1976.
When Children Ask about Sex. New York: Meredith Press, 1969.

CHAPTER 6
THE PROMISING POTENTIAL OF RELIGIOUS INSTITUTIONS

For many years, parents and community professionals have recognized the important influence of religious institutions in shaping values and in communicating about moral and ethical issues. Religious institutions traditionally have supported the family and have offered support of various kinds to families facing stress and hardship.

In recent years, religious leaders also have examined their denominations' teachings and interpreted them to the community in light of the changing times. Priests, ministers, and rabbis are highly respected for their compassion, wisdom, and their involvement in community and family issues.

Human sexuality is mentioned in many contexts in religious teachings. However, many family members have difficulty interpreting biblical passages as guidelines for their own behavior. The efforts by some denominations to identify human sexuality as an area of concern have resulted in creative and well-attended programs sponsored by religious institutions. The real strength of such programs is their emphasis on family involvement. Sessions are frequently designed for parents and youth to attend together. Assignments between sessions involve opening channels of communication between parents and their children. Religious teachings are interpreted and clarified in terms of current lifestyles and sexual practices. By communicating to the congregation that religious teachings are relevant to human sexuality, religious leaders can encourage family members to seek counseling and education before sexual issues result in family problems.

Some religious leaders, when asked why they don't conduct discussion groups or educational sessions on sexual issues, replied by saying that no one asked them to. This assumes that a need must be verbalized in order to gain recognition as legitimate. A far better measure of legitimacy is the response of the congregation once discussion sessions are offered. Rabbis, ministers, and priests must not wait for members of their congregations to initiate action around the need for sexual learning. Religious leaders must assume leadership in offering learning opportunities in human sexuality.

For those religious leaders who are uncertain how to initiate discussion groups, several options are available:

1. If the uncertainty is rooted in a discomfort about discussing sexual matters, then it will be most helpful to involve others in this effort. Perhaps the religious leader would initially be most comfortable moderating a panel of persons who present a variety of perspectives on human sexuality. Perhaps a series of guest discussion leaders would help community residents become acquainted with local resources. Perhaps the leader could select a co-leader who is both comfortable and knowledgeable about sexual concerns of individuals across the life cycle. Working with such a person promotes a sharing of effort that enables each co-leader to do what he/she does best. A compatible co-leader might be identified from the congregation or might be a community person who would welcome the opportunity to help the religious institution become more involved in offering guidance in the area of sexual learning.

2. If the religious leader is basically comfortable with the topic of human sexuality, but not especially confident that he/she could handle factual questions that might arise, several avenues are open. First, there are many good books on sexuality representing a variety of perspectives. Increasing one's knowledge base through reading will fuel self-confidence and also provide the religious leader with readings to recommend to family members who wish to learn more once the sessions are underway.

   Second, a knowledgeable co-leader will undoubtedly prove helpful in assisting with group discussion, since working with a group requires both energy and a knowledge base.

   Lastly, if a member of the group does ask a question that the religious leader cannot answer, he/she can acknowledge the difficulty of the question and inquire whether anyone in the group can provide an answer. If not, then the leader should offer to consult available resources and identify an answer for discussion at the next session. Although it might seem as though an admission of ignorance

66

could threaten the group's confidence in the leader, it is far more likely that members will feel relief that the leader is human and not all-knowing. The religious leader at the same time serves as a good role model for adults who realize that there are resources they can consult to gain needed knowledge.

3. Some religious leaders may, for a variety of reasons, be reluctant to initiate discussion groups about sexuality with members of their congregation. If this is the case, the most beneficial alternative would be to identify groups and organizations in the community that family members could utilize to explore their questions and concerns about sexuality.

Regardless of what level of activity the religious leader decides to pursue to help members of the congregation to increase their sexual learning, it is especially important, concurrently, to support community efforts in that direction. The support may take the form of active participation on community panels, of writing letters to the local newspaper, of supporting school board action in favor of sex education, or of helping community members recognize the appropriateness of expanding their sexual learning beyond that offered from a religious perspective.

Several religious organizations sponsoring projects in human sexuality provide examples of creative endeavors at the community level. The United Church of Christ, through its "Neighbors In Need" (NIN) Teenage Pregancy Project, has provided financial grants to a variety of programs. Funded projects have included Casa Central, an inner-city Hispanic community outreach center in Chicago, which has used grant money to hire an outreach worker to develop educational programs in responsible sexuality; the Philadelphia Men's Resource Center, which sponsored a program of father and son weekend workshops aimed at encouraging male teenagers to make reponsible sexual decisions; and the South and Central Washington/North Idaho Conferences which have trained one adult and one young person from each of sixteen congregations in order to offer separate sexuality programs for adults and youth.

The Unitarian Universalist Association developed the multimedia curriculum "About Your Sexuality" in 1971. Originally designed for adolescents between ages twelve and fourteen, the program has also been used with older teenagers and with adults. Other religious groups, Planned Parenthoods, colleges, and a variety of social service agencies have used the program. It treats issues not traditionally covered in school programs. Teaching aids, instructional booklets, activity sheets, and audiovisual materials are provided on the subjects of masturbation, "making out," making love, homosexual life-styles, as well as on birth control, veneral disease, femininity and masculinity, male and female anatomy, same-sex relationships, conception, and childbirth. The package, which contains enough material for thirty or forty one-and-one-half hour sessions, is intended for use in small discussion groups which are led by a male and female team. Parents are always asked for their permission for a child to participate. Evaluations of 800 program participants indicated that they became less "confused" about thirteen topic areas; more frequently discussed the topics with parents, friends, and others; and became more tolerant of variation in sexual expression. The most significant increase in communication occurred with members of the immediate family — particularly the father.

Catholic Alternatives provides counseling and educational services on such topics as birth control, sexual decision making, venereal disease, abortion, and sterilization. Begun in 1976 as a counseling center on sexuality, Catholic Alternatives offers an aggressive outreach program to young people, including Hispanic youth. All materials, counseling services, and other contacts are available in Spanish and English. One major outreach effort is a series of "Sexual Responsibility Workshops," which covers such topics as teenage relationships with parents and each other, physiology, teen parenting, pregnancy prevention, adoption and abortion, and venereal disease. Videotapes and newsletters have also been produced and distributed by trained teen interns recruited to expand the outreach efforts of Catholic Alternatives.

Religious efforts in education, counseling, and values clarification are of great importance to parents and young people alike. The function of most religious education is to provide a forum for exploration of pressing issues in everyday life, including human sexuality. Whether through aggressive outreach programs, personal counseling, educational forums, or participation in community-wide sexual learning efforts, religious institutions and their leaders face an opportunity and a challenge to help adults and young people become more knowledgeable and comfortable with their sexual values in today's society.

Resource Materials

Benziger Family Life Program. Encino, California: Benziger, Inc.

Borowitz, E.B. *Choosing a Sex Ethic: A Jewish Inquiry*. New York: Schocken Books, 1969.

Calderone, M.S. *Human Sexuality and the Quaker Conscience*. Philadelphia: Friends Book Store, 1973.

Calderwood, D. *About Your Sexuality*. Boston: Unitarian — Universalist Association, 1978. A multimedia program for junior high levels and up. $135.00.

The Catholic Sex Manual for Teenagers. Albuquerque, New Mexico: The American Classical Press.

Daum, A., and Strongin, B. *Course on Human Sexuality for Adolescents in Religious Schools, Youth Groups, and Camps*. New York: New York Federation of Reform Synagogues, 1979.

Feldman, D. *Marital Relations, Birth Control, and Abortion in Jewish Law*. New York: Schocken Books, 1974.

Friends Home Service Committee. *Towards a Quaker View of Sex*. Philadelphia: Friends Book Store, 1964.

Genné, W.H. *A Synoptic of Recent Denominational Statements on Sexuality*. New York: National Council of Churches, 1976.

Gittelsohn, R.B. *Love, Sex and Marriage: A Jewish View*. New York: Union of American Hebrew Congregations, 1980.

Gordis, R. *Love and Sex: A Modern Jewish Perspective*. New York: Farrar, Strauss, and Giroux, 1978.

Hambrick-Stowe, E. *Expecting*. Valley Forge, Pennsylvania: Judson Press, 1974.

Human Sexuality – New Directions in American Catholic Thought. Ramsey, New Jersey: The Paulist Press, 1977.

Keane, P.S. *Sexual Morality: A Catholic Perspective*. Ramsey, New Jersey: The Paulist Press, 1977.

Kennedy, E. *What A Modern Catholic Believes about Sex*. Chicago: The Thomas More Press, 1971.

Lutheran Church Press. *Understanding Your Sexual Self*. Philadelphia: Fortress Church Supply Stores, 1979. For grades 8-9.

Lutheran Church Press. *Update on Love, Sex, and Life*. Philadelphia: Fortress Church Supply Stores, 1974. For senior high level.

Mace, D. *The Christian Response to the Sexual Revolution*. Nashville, Tennessee: Abingdon Press, 1970.

Minor, H. W., Myskens, J.B., and Alexander, M.N. *Sex Education – The Schools and* the Churches. Richmond, Virginia: John Knox Press, 1971.

Problem Pregnancies: Toward a Responsible Decision. New York: The United Presbyterian Church in the United States of America, 1978.

Rabinowitz, S. *A Jewish View of Love and Marriage.* Washington, D.C. B'nai B'rith Youth Organization, 1972.

Sexuality and the Human Community. New York: United Presbyterian Church, 1970.

Tierney, J. Sex education books for children. *Catholic Library World,* May-June, *42:* 567-570, 1971

United Church of Christ. *Human Sexuality: A Preliminary Study.* New York: Pilgrim Press, 1977, pp. 103-105.

Webb, M. *Family Planning: Emerging Issues and Christian Perspectives.* New York: National Council of Churches, 1972.

CHAPTER 7

CHANGE THROUGH SCHOOL-COMMUNITY COOPERATION

In the area of human sexuality there is a particular need to develop programs that involve many segments of the community: schools need to be aware of local resources to aid them in program and curriculum, development and their board members must be convinced of the importance of incorporating age-appropriate information on human sexuality into the curriculum at all grade levels; parents must be encouraged to offer their input and support as well as to improve their own comfort and competence as sex educators; community resources must identify gaps and inadequacies in the provision of sexual learning at all stages of the life cycle.

Because of the controversy that surrounds ''sex education'' in many communities, it is especially important to develop sufficient parental and community support to expand and improve both traditional and innovative efforts. School involvement by no means takes away from the roles of parents and religious institutions in contributing to the sexual learning of young people of all ages. Rather, schools can serve as a support for already existing efforts and, in some cases, school participation in this area may even serve as a catalyst for parents and other community resources to become more purposeful in their roles as sex educators.

Efforts to develop and expand sexual learning opportunities have often foundered or failed because involved participants did not pay sufficient attention to building a core of support and to keeping pace with the community's readiness for change. Persons interested in developing new progams or curricula concerned with sexual learning need to lay careful groundwork, to be satisfied with small initial steps, to seek school and community involvement, to elicit constant feedback, and to utilize a wide range of expertise already present in the community. It is hoped that the sequence of community organization principles presented in this chapter can provide guidelines for persons or groups wishing to

71

improve the quality of sexual learning available in their schools and communities.

Locating Existing Resources

Identifying ongoing programs and providers of sexual learning are important initial steps in the process of assessing community needs and readiness for further sex education efforts. Current providers of sex education can offer information regarding ideas for new directions, anticipated sources of opposition, level of satisfaction with existing programs, and available resources (professional, financial and media) for further sex education efforts.

Gathering this information can be one of the first steps toward recruiting persons to serve on an advisory board. Sources of existing programs might include:

Community	*Schools*
local hospitals	principals
family planning agencies	health teachers
youth bureaus	home economics teachers
4-H Clubs	science teachers
Cooperative Extensions	social studies teachers
public health	school nurse
VD treatment clinics	school social worker
crisis or rape counseling services	school psychologist
family counseling	PTA
mental health services	community resources
religious institutions	
school programs or curricula	

Just as community agencies need to be aware of programs and curricula offered through the schools, educators should be knowledgeable about existing community resources. In cooperative school-community efforts there should be a ready interchange and sharing of resources. Agencies can provide guest speakers and media resources to school programs; schools can provide space and publicity for community programs as well as concerned professionals to serve on community advisory committees.

Sizing Up The Opposition

Not everyone concerned about sex education in the school or community can be considered supportive of efforts to expand sex education efforts. Identifying potential sources of opposition is crucial for two reasons: (1) to gauge their reasons for opposing expanded sex education efforts; and (2) to assess the strength of their opposition. Clearly, in this exploratory phase, contacts with conservative forces will not result in program opposition per se, but will enable concerned school and community persons to inform themselves in advance of potential areas of concern. Persons opposed to sex education often have similar objections to specific programs:

a. They question the qualifications of the teacher or program leader. This stems from the concern that their children be taught by a knowledgeable professional who also possesses the skills to facilitate group discussions on sensitive topics. Knowledge of the training and experience of the leader is often sufficient to reassure persons who have special concerns in this area.

b. They feel excluded from the process of program or curriculum development, or, at the very least, from being provided with program objectives, resources to be used, and an opportunity to discuss program efforts with an involved staff member. Involving these persons in various stages of program planning and implementation can provide opportunities for them to raise concerns, to offer input and to be knowledgeable about the final product of the group effort. If ongoing involvement is not feasible, then an open house or community forum to discuss the new program and to obtain community input is advisable before initiating the program.

c. Some parents believe that their role as sex educators of their children is being usurped by the new program. These parents often feel very hesitant in providing sex education to their children, and many would be responsive to a parent discussion/education group to help them with such concerns. Other parents who are comfortable in discussing sexual issues with their children want to be certain that their children learn *first* in the home and later from other school or community programs. For these parents, an awareness of the material to be taught or discussed in the proposed

73

program enables them to introduce the pertinent topics at home in advance of the program's schedule.

d. Some community members are opposed to the notion that values clarification and decision-making skills are an integral component of some sex education programs. These opponents of sex education believe that all young people need to know about certain matters (masturbation, homosexuality, abortion, premarital intercourse) is that such activities are morally wrong. Individuals holding these beliefs see the use of values clarification as undermining the parent's role as transmitter of values by encouraging children to question those values. Many opponents of sex education on moral grounds would be more comfortable having their religious institution provide sexual learning and guidance for young people, since a religious perspective is more likely to be compatible with their moral convictions than is an effort that helps adolescents explore which values and ethics are best suited to their own personal life situations.

Developing An Advisory Committee

The purpose of an advisory committee is to develop broad-based support, to draw upon the expertise and concern of members, and to marshall a source of energy for future program development efforts. Whether this committee is appointed (perhaps by the school board, the PTA, or by a core of concerned community members) or is selected from volunteers (knowledgeable school or agency staff members, concerned parents), it is crucial that the committee should:

— represent a broad perspective of the community to be served by new programs in terms of race, income, occupation, and geographic region. It is especially important to have a good representation of parents and adolescents.

— respond to issues of policy and program implementation.

— bring community concerns for consideration by the advisory committee.

— develop good public relations by involving the media to mobilize interest and support for new and proposed programs in the community.

74

Conducting a Needs Assessment

An initial task of an advisory committee is to gather information that can be used to justify later program directions. In identifying the needs of the specific community, or a target group in the community, it may be important to gather pertinent statistics from community agencies on problems relating to sexuality and premature parenthood. This information subsequently can be used in discussions with school or community persons who try to deny the seriousness of sexual concerns faced by local young people. Agencies having access to helpful information include:

A. Planned Parenthood, Family Planning, or Public Health
   1. number of teenagers served
   2. number of pregnant adolescents
   3. resolution of pregnancy (miscarriage, abortion, carried to term)
B. Public Health
   1. VD rate among adolescents as compared to persons age 20 and over
   2. state health statistics on adolescents as compared to adolescents in specific counties
   3. birth defects of babies born to adolescent mothers as compared to mothers 20 and over.
C. Public Schools
   1. number of female students leaving school because of pregnancy
   2. number of female students who return to school following a pregnancy, including subsequent dropout rate
   3. number of females in special programs for pregnant students
D. County Department of Social Services
   1. number of parents under age 20 receiving public assistance, food stamps, or Medicaid
   2. rate of child abuse or neglect for adolescent parents

Data Analysis

Once the advisory committee has determined areas of need, it is necessary to identify long range program goals, to prioritize these goals,

75

and to develop specific program objectives. At this time it is especially important to consider the likelihood of community approval for any proposed programs. It is far better to begin with a small, well supported program that addresses a recognized need than it is to move ahead of the community's pace with a program that is controversial or not well appreciated. Examples of long-term goals can vary widely in comprehensiveness and sophistication:

— incorporating material on human sexuality into an existing family life education curriculum
— developing a program to help parents become more comfortable and competent sex educators
— increasing cooperation between community resources and school needs
— encouraging local agencies with programs in sexual learning to make their programs more responsive to the needs of males
— developing a peer counseling program
— developing a teamwork approach with other school professionals as certain material relating to sexuality is taught in each of several courses
— working with local clergy to encourage them to develop a family approach to sexual learning
— building a comprehensive K-12 education curriculum that includes age-appropriate material on sexuality
— developing a pamphlet of resource persons in the community who are available to conduct workshops, be guest speakers, or serve as consultants on topics relating to human sexuality

Each of the long-range goals should in turn be broken down into specific objectives. This enables members of the advisory committee to share responsibility for various objectives. It also permits realistic planning in terms of sequencing, time frames, and building community support on a gradual basis.

Raising Community Awareness

One important aspect of building a program is to be certain that the community perceives a need for the program. When proposed programs are in the area of human sexuality, there is a special need for sensitivity

76

by program developers, given the concerns and suspicions many people have about sexual learning.

The best approach is to emphasize that sexuality is a natural and normal part of a person's maturation and development, and that regardless of parents' preferences many young people will choose to become sexually active. Although abstinence can be presented as a desirable alternative in any sex education program, such a program should also prepare young people to make informed decisions, to protect themselves against pregnancy and sexually transmitted diseases, and to become aware of potential consequences of sexual activity.

Raising community awareness can occur in several ways:

— a series of newspaper articles citing statistics relating to problematic consequences of adolescent sexuality. Some anonymous or hypothetical case studies can add personal impact to the statistics. The articles should stress "what needs to be done," which could include educational programs, curriculum revision, agency efforts, parent involvement, or whatever other continuing steps are appropriate for a given community. Although the newspaper journalist will prefer to write the articles, he/she will undoubtedly welcome any statistics gathered that relate to problematic aspects or consequences of adolescent sexuality.

— a community workshop can serve the dual purpose of informing community residents about the extent of problems relating to adolescent sexuality and can also be the beginning step for continuing involvement as ongoing committees are formed. It will be extremely useful to have multi-agency sponsorship for this workshop, as this allows for sharing in the initial planning stages and for inter-agency cooperation in whatever continuing activities result from the workshop.

— appearances on radio or television talk shows. Although a respected community person can be influential in sharing information and proposing programs, a series of speakers or panel presentations can present a broader perspective and also eliminate the possibility of identifying concerns as belonging to one individual in isolation.

— programs or panel presentations at PTA meetings or at other

77

groups which attract parents (Parents Without Partners, Parents Anonymous, advisory committees of Scouts, 4-H Clubs, youth bureaus, etc.)

Efforts to raise community awareness should be accomplished by seeking concurrent input from community members. If the advisory committee has misjudged the readiness of the community, or if specific components of a new program raise strong objections, this information should be taken into account before proceeding with the original plans.

Program Development and Implementation

Once school and community attitudes have been expressed and support has been generated for the goals and objectives of the proposed program, it is important to consider the unique learning needs of the target group to be served by the program. If possible, members of the target group should be encouraged to give input regarding their needs to the advisory or planning committee.

In the early meetings with the target group, an effort should be made to communicate broad program goals and to elicit participants' requests for specific content, skills, or information. This can be done verbally or by having each participant complete a questionnaire designed to measure the extent of his or her current learning. Once the program is underway, ongoing feedback from the target group should be elicited periodically so that the leader can remain responsive to the participants' needs.

Evaluation

Evaluation criteria should be based on the stated goals of the program. Ideally, participants should be asked to complete several instruments designed to measure the extent of new learning during their participation in the program. Some very good instruments for use with adolescents are available through MATHTECH in Bethesda, Maryland (1979). If possible, participants should be asked to complete the instrument before the program begins, at the conclusion of the program, and at a follow-up session several months later. Such measures will provide useful information regarding the extent to which new learning is acquired and maintained over time. Other desirable conditions to strive for during evaluation planning include random selection of participants and selection of a control group.

At the very least, the evaluation should serve the purpose of providing feedback regarding the knowledge or skills possessed by the participants at the conclusion of the program. More sophisticated evaluations may allow the evaluator to make specific claims about the gains that participants can attribute to the program and, further, may enable the evaluator to generalize the findings beyond the specific participants in the program.

Many evaluations also seek to measure the level of satisfaction that participants feel at the conclusion of the program. Since most program leaders try to create an atmosphere of acceptance, confidence, trust, and support, it is understandable that they would value feedback on affective as well as cognitive responses by participants.

Building Ongoing School-Community Support

Once the evaluation results are analyzed, advisory group members and leaders will have specific feedback regarding their success in achieving specific objectives. Subsequent programs may be modified based on existing program inadequacies, newly identified needs, and availability of additional resources.

Beyond specific program planning efforts, it is important to keep up good public relations efforts through the media, the advisory committee, and local community awareness projects. Failure to keep the community informed of ongoing program efforts leaves new programs vulnerable to attack by persons who can expect the community to believe inaccurate rumors or half-truths. Accurate publicity of current program efforts is a program's best defense against attack.

The advisory committee should constantly be searching for new resource people to assist in school and community efforts. Although it is wise to strive for some new membership, it is desirable to keep a portion of the membership stable over time so that the committee can maintain a sense of continuity in its efforts.

An advisory group must constantly be available and accessible to work with other planning and advisory groups in the schools and in the community who wish to initiate or expand programs to promote sexual learning. School and community advisory committees can offer mutual support to one another in their efforts to improve the quality of sexual learning available in many community environments. The community will determine the pace at which change can occur, which is why community involvement and commitment are so critical to any change effort. To ignore the community will not cause resistance to disappear; instead it will slow the change effort or even encourage active resistance to plans made without community input. However, achieving community input does not mean that the community person's *first* effort is to organize a workshop, make a presentation before the school board, or appear on a local television program. Good groundwork is at the root of the most successful projects in community change. Part of the groundwork involves the participation of other concerned persons who can share the work, the frustrations *and* the satisfactions of any change effort.

Service gaps in the area of human sexuality exist in every community. Once one assumes a lifespan approach to the concept of sexual learning, a wide range of possible projects springs to mind: perhaps the local family service agency is offering classes to help parents communicate with their adolescents about sexual issues, but no groups are being developed for parents of younger children; perhaps the focus on helping parents has been so extensive that adults who are not parents have been ignored as they struggle with sexual issues; perhaps the local probation department is so preoccupied with the delinquent acts of its adolescent clients that its workers never consider that confusion or inadequate knowledge about sexuality may be a concern for the teen on probation — as is the case with most adolescents.

With broad segments of the community interested in learning about various aspects of human sexuality, the concept of participant broadens to include parents, youth workers, agency staff, clergy, and all other interested school staff and community residents who recognize that sexual learning occurs constantly throughout the life cycle. Only by being comfortable with ourselves as sexual beings can we help young people to accept sexuality as a normal and natural aspect of their physical and emotional development.

REFERENCES

Kirby, D., Alter, J., and Scales, P. *An Analysis of United States Sex Education Programs and Evaluation Methods.* Bethesda, Maryland: MATHTECH, Inc., 1979.

Resource Materials

American School Health Association. *Growth Patterns and Sex Education: A Suggested Program for Kindergarten through Grade Twelve.* Kent, Ohio: American School Health Association, 1974.

Bradshaw, B.R., Wolfe, W.M., Wood, T.J., and Tyler L.S. *Counseling on Family Planning and Human Sexuality.* New York: Family Service Association of America, 1977.

Brill-Lehn, S. *Sex Education: A Resource and Strategy Guide for California Communities.* Washington, D.C.: The Population Institute, 1976.

Broderick, C., and Bernard, J. (Eds.): *The Individual, Sex and Society: A SIECUS Handbook for Teachers and Counselors.* Baltimore: The Johns Hopkins Press, 1969.

Burt, J., and Meeks, L. *Education for Sexuality: Concepts and Programs for Teaching.* Philadelphia: W.B. Saunders Co., 1975.

Calderone, M. *The Family Book about Sexuality.* Philadelphia: Lippincott/Crowell, 1980.

California State Department of Education. *Framework for Health Instruction In California Public Schools: Kindergarten to Grade Twelve.* Sacramento, California: California State Department of Education, 1972.

California Youth Authority. *Family Life Education Curriculum Guide.* Sacramento, California: California Youth Authority, 1974.

Commission of Professional Rights and Responsibilities. *Suggestions for Defense against Extremist Attack: Sex Education in the Public Schools.* Washington, D.C.: National Education Association, 1970.

Dodds, J.M. *Human Sexuality: A Curriculum for Teens.* Rochester, New York: Planned Parenthood of Rochester and Monroe County, 1979.

Eggleston, A.P., and Connolly, N. *Understanding Human Sexuality: Teaching Modules for Educators.* Ithaca, New York: New York State College of Human Ecology, Cornell University, 1980.

Family Life and Human Development, Sample Units K-6. Upper Marlboro, Maryland: Prince George's County Public Schools, 1977.

Family Life Education, Resource Guide, Grades 1-12. Wilmington, Delaware: Wilmington Public Schools, 1969.

The Fine Art of Parenting: A PTA Priority. Chicago: National PTA, 700 N. Rush St., Chicago, Illinois.

Gordon, S., and Dickman, I. *Schools and Parents – Partners in Sex Education.* New York: Public Affairs Pamphlets, 381 Park Avenue, South, 1980.

Grams, A. *Sex Education: A Guide for Teachers and Parents.* Danville, Illinois: Interstate Printers and Publishers, Inc., 1969.

Haims, L. J. *Sex Education and the Public Schools: A Multi-Dimensional Study for the 1970s.* Toronto: Lexington Books, 1973.

Hawley, N. *Project Teen Concern.* San Francisco: Planned Parenthood Alameda — San Francisco, 1978.

Hinton, J.D. *Teaching Sex Education: A Guide for Teachers.* Palo Alto, California: Fearon Publishers, 1969.

Hottois, J., and Milner, N. *The Sex Education Controversy: A Resource and Strategy Guide for California Communities.* Washington, D.C.: The Population Institute, 1976.

Institute for Family Research and Education. *Community Family Life Education Program for Parents: A Training Manual for Organizers.* Charlottesville, Virginia: Ed-U-Press, 1977.

Kempton, W. *Techniques for Leading Group Discussions on Human Sexuality.* Charlottesville, Virginia: Ed-U-Press, 1973.

Kilander, F.H. *Sex Education in the Schools: A Study of Objectives, Content, Methods, Materials and Evaluation.* New York: The MacMillan Company, 1970.

Kirkendall, L., and Osborne, R.F. *Teacher's Question-and-Answer Book on Sex Education.* New London, Connecticut: Croft Educational Services, 1970.

Lang, J. *Curriculum Guides for Family Life and Sex Education: An Annotated Bibliography.* Portland, Oregon: E.C. Brown Foundation, 1972.

Morrison, E.S., and Price, M.W. *Values in Sexuality: A New Approach to Sex Education.* New York: Hart Publishing Company, 1974.

National Council on Family Relations. *High School Exchange: Resources for Teaching about Family Life Education.* Minneapolis, Minnesota: National Council on Family Relations, 1976.

Pappalardo, J. *A Guide to Values Clarification in Sex Education.* Cleveland, Ohio: PRETERM Institute, 1978.

Perrin, M., and Smith, T. *Ideas and Learning Activities for Family Life and Sex Education.* Dubuque, Iowa: Wm. C. Brown Co., Publishers, 1972.

Roberts, E. (Ed.): *Childhood Sexual Learning: The Unwritten Curriculum.* Cambridge, Massachusetts: Ballinger Publishing Co., 1980.

Scales, P. *Sex Education and the Prevention of Teenage Pregnancy – An Overview of Policies and Programs in the United States.* Washington, D.C.: The Family Impact Seminar, 1979.

Scales, P. *Teenage Pregnancy: A Selected Bibliography.* Baltimore: National Alliance for Optional Parenthood, 1978.

Schiller, P. *Creative Approach to Sex Education and Counseling.* New York: Association Press, 1974.

Schultz, E.D., and Williams, S.R. *Family Life and Sex Education: Curriculum and Instruction.* New York: Harcourt Brace and World, Inc., 1968.

Sex Education: A Working Design for Curriculum Development and Implementation – Grades Pre-kindergarten through Twelve. Mineola, New York: Education Council for School Research and Development, 1968.

Sex Information and Education Council of the United States. *Human Sexuality: A*

Selected Bibliography for Professionals. New York: Human Sciences Press, 1978.

Shapiro, C.H. *Adolescent Pregnancy Prevention: A Team Approach.* Ithaca, New York: Department of Human Service Studies, 1979.

SIECUS. *Film Resources for Sex Education.* New York: Sex Information and Education Council of the United States, 1971.

Singer, L.J., and Buskin, J. *Sex Education on Film: A Guide to Visual Aids and Programs.* New York: Teacher's College Press, 1971.

Somerville, R.M. *Introduction to Family Life and Sex Education.* Englewood Cliffs, New Jersey: Prentice-Hall, Inc., 1972.

Youth and Student Affairs. *A Guide to Sexuality Handbooks: Sex Education Resources.* New York: Planned Parenthood Federation of America, Inc.

CHAPTER 8

BIRTH CONTROL AND SEXUALLY TRANSMITTED DISEASES

Rosalind Kenworthy
Constance Hoenk Shapiro

Adolescents are often uninformed about two crucial aspects of sexual intimacy: *pregnancy prevention* and *sexually transmitted diseases*. Ignorance or denial is especially dangerous when an adolescent is confronted with symptoms suggestive of pregnancy or STD, since a delay in seeking medical care or counseling may have serious consequences. For this reason, this chapter will summarize the facts that a professional may need to know and to impart to young people who are learning about their sexuality and responsible decision making.

It has been said that the only 100 percent effective form of birth control is the word "no." As adolescents face peer pressure, satisfy their curiosity, try to act "grown up," and become aware of compelling sexual feelings, they do not always anticipate how to respond in situations where the temptation for sexual activity is great. In a 1976 study by Cvetkovich and Grote, females reported becoming sexually involved because they couldn't say no, because they wanted to please and satisfy their boyfriends, or because it seemed as though sexual activity was expected of them. In the same study, males reported experiencing difficulty and embarrassment in discussing contraception with their female partners. Clearly, new skills in addition to factual knowledge are necessary so that adolescents can cope with bodily changes and the prospect of new interpersonal relationships.

Adolescents often exhibit a façade of being knowledgcable and experienced when the topic of sex arises. However, in many cases, even those adolescents who have knowledge of anatomy are not aware of the practical considerations or consequences that accompany sexual activity. Between ignorance and myths about sexuality, teenagers are often confused and ill-informed about their bodies and the risks of pregnancy and venereal disease. A 1979 New York City study by Ross noted that students in biology, health, and/or sex education classes are no more knowledgeable than friends who had not take such courses. The researchers speculated that this reflected the typical curriculum of such courses — focusing on what connects to what — rather than providing useful information.

Although adolescents need to know facts, they need help in using these facts to assist them in understanding their bodies, in making decisions, and in protecting themselves against pregnancy and venereal disease. Human service professionals can use a variety of creative approaches and resources in helping teenagers to link facts with behaviors and the consequences of behaviors. The use of role plays and simulated case studies can encourage both behavioral rehearsal and thoughtful discussion. Facts coupled with real-life implications may in turn help adolescents to form attitudes and codes of conduct that will guide them in future interactions with their peers and family members. Schinke and Gilchrist (1977) suggest that interpersonal communication skill training may represent an important step in helping adolescents deal with their sexuality and contraceptive behavior. In a study they conducted, ten students participated in four 2-hour group training sessions led by two social workers. A typical training session began with a brief description of effective ways of presenting oneself in a variety of interpersonal situations.

Leaders modeled competent responses, emphasizing eye contact, body posture, gestures, voice volume, fluency, affect, and positive self-statements. Students were then asked to role play sample responses, receiving feedback and reinforcement from other students and the leaders. Students were encouraged to express their feelings honestly and openly, refuse any unreasonable requests, and assert themselves in a convincing manner. Student participation in group training sessions was marked by active involvement of everyone in attendance. Role plays and practices were extremely popular, with most students reporting that they used the learned interpersonal skills outside of the training sessions. Many related successful interactions in previously problematic situations with friends and family.

Young people may be asked to submit examples of problematic situations for role play or group discussion purposes. Other examples

85

may be obtained from books such as Sol Gordon's *You Would If You Loved Me (1978)*, a collection of actual "lines" commonly used by young men and women to seduce their peers. Dr. Gordon wrote this book in the belief that familiarizing young people with typical "lines," as well as possible responses, would help them to cope with peer pressure and to articulate their needs and values clearly.

Role plays and sample "lines" are especially valuable to use in learning environments with both male and female participants, since young people can be sensitized to the feelings of their peers and can be helped to support one another in honest and open discussions about their sexuality.

Helping teenagers to use "no" as a 100 percent effective method of birth control will be the goal of many teachers, parents, and community professionals. However, some adolescents will choose to become sexually active or will succumb to pressure. For those adolescents, facts about contraception and venereal disease are of immediate relevance. The factual information should be presented in such a way that adolescents can relate it to their personal (or prospective) life situations.

For the unmarried adolescent, there are certain considerations which complicate the decision-making process related to contraception. A primary consideration is that of embarrassment. Adolescents who want to maintain some privacy about their sexual activities may be quite reluctant to purchase contraceptives from a neighborhood drugstore or to seek birth control information and devices from their family physicians. In addition to the embarrassment of facing adults whom they fear will condemn their contemplated sexual activity, adolescents must also deal with the nagging apprehension that their parents will discover the contraceptive device. Even to enter a family planning clinic is too embarrassing for the adolescent who fears an encounter with adult acquaintances. Vending machines for condoms owe their success largely to the adolescent's wish to preserve the privacy of his sexual activities. Another form of embarrassment may be anticipated at the awkwardness in front of one's partner of using contraceptive methods such as foam or condoms.

A consideration for the adolescent female relates to stereotypical ideas that have been communicated during her youth. A young woman using contraception may feel that she will be rejected or ridiculed by her partner for taking an active role in the sexual relationship despite social conditioning to be passive. Also relating to society's double standard is the feeling by females that their use of contraception may cause their partners to feel that they have "been around."

Another consideration is that of spontaneity. For the teenager who engages in sexual activity infrequently or sporadically, the need to plan ahead and prepare requires a very realistic assessment of the consequences of sexual activity. Some adolescents avoid such planning because they don't want to appear as if they were prepared for, or expecting to have, sex.

Few methods of birth control are without disadvantages for the adolescent. Although the effectiveness of the pill would make it seem highly desirable for the adolescent female, for the many young women whose sexual activity is occasional or sporadic, the expense and need to take the pill daily may seem undesirable. The intrauterine device (IUD) eliminates the need for daily remembering, but it is more difficult for doctors to insert this device in women who have not had children, and there is a greater likelihood of complications in the never-pregnant female. The inconvenience of the diaphragm is a potential drawback for the adolescent who finds it awkward to carry with her to places where sexual activity is likely to occur. For multiple acts of intercourse, the reapplication of spermicide by itself or in conjunction with a diaphragm may be an unwelcome interruption in sexual activity for the adolescent female, just as unrolling a condom may be for the adolescent male. If used alone, condoms are about 80 percent dependable in preventing conception and also provide protection against venereal disease. Some males complain that they interfere with physical pleasure and sexual spontaneity.

The belief by some adolescents that contraception interferes physically or psychologically with sexual pleasure causes some to prefer to take risks, and in some cases the awareness of risk adds a tantalizing element to the adolescent's feeling of indulging in forbidden experiences. When weighing the inconveniences of obtaining and using birth control against the seemingly remote consequences of taking a chance and getting pregnant (or causing someone to get pregnant), many adolescents will opt to take a chance.

Adolescent pregnancy prevention rests heavily on the capacity of sexually active adolescents to engage in anticipatory thinking and decision making. The factual information in the remainder of this chapter is a first step in the knowledge base that adolescents must develop as they weigh the risks and consequences of unprotected sexual activity against the inconvenience and potential embarrassment of using a dependable method of contraception.

Dependable Methods of Birth Control

The Diaphragm

HOW IT WORKS. The diaphragm is a shallow rubber cup with a flexible rim which holds spermicidal jelly or cream against the cervix. Some sperm are deflected by the diaphragm; those that swim around it are immobilized by the spermicide. The diaphragm without cream or jelly is not dependable. It is inserted into the vagina up to two hours before genital contact (including intercourse) occurs, and it must remain in place eight hours after the last episode of intercourse because sperm can live in the vagina for eight hours. Protection is dependable for only one ejaculation. If intercourse is repeated within eight hours, the diaphragm is left in place. To maintain dependable contraception, additional spermicide is inserted with an applicator or a condom may be used.

Diaphragms come in different sizes and must be fitted by a clinician during an internal pelvic exam. The vagina is very elastic and sensitive to physical and psychological stimuli. A clinician may need to check the diaphragm several times before the correct size is ascertained. If it feels uncomfortable to the wearer or her partner, it has been improperly inserted or incorrectly fitted.

BENEFITS. The diaphragm has become a popular method of contraception, largely because it has rare, minimal side effects. Another significant advantage is that it is used only when it is needed so that it is usually appropriate for people who require contraception only occasionally.

RISKS. Even when correctly used every time a couple has intercourse, a diaphragm has about a 5 percent failure rate. This means that a couple depending on the diaphragm should carefully consider their possible responses to pregnancy.

Sexual responses inhibit rational controlled behavior. Use of the diaphragm depends on control. The result for some people is that sexual spontaneity distracts them from using the diaphragm every time. For others, sexual responses are depressed by conscientious use of the contraceptive. The problem can be solved, but it often requires practice and patience. Some women have found that teaching their partners how to insert and check the diaphragm has been a significant factor in its being used correctly every time; both partners learn how to integrate rational control with sexual response rather than letting one impinge on the other.

Diaphragm use is associated with urinary tract infections for a few women; repeated attacks can be a serious problem and may force a woman to consider alternative methods.

The Pill

HOW IT WORKS. A second pregnancy can't begin when a woman is already pregnant. The pill prevents pregnancy in essentially the same way that the normal hormonal changes of pregnancy insure only one pregnancy at a time: by inhibiting the ovary from releasing a mature egg. "The pill" (there are 20-30 kinds) is composed of synthetic forms of estrogen and progesterone, both of which are normally present in fluctuating amounts. Taking a pill every day keeps a steady level of each hormone, thus "fooling" the ovary, and providing contraceptive protection at all times. It is not, however, a flexible method for people who sometimes abstain. Stopping the pill for longer than the normal week's break between cycles means a woman has to wait for a normal menstrual period to start it again. Stopping is not advised unless a woman wants to get pregnant, or has another form of contraception, or knows she will abstain from any sexual activity for more than 3-6 months. A few months' interruption of the pill provides no medical benefits, means a woman's body must readjust to it when she starts it again, and results in a number of unwanted pregnancies. Therefore, some doctors recommend that every woman receiving the pill be provided with a second method of birth control and instructions in the use of that method.

Appointments for pill prescriptions can be made at family planning clinics or with a private physician.

BENEFITS. The pill is the most dependable contraceptive available.

89

When properly used, it is the only method of birth control which is nearly 100 percent dependable. For many couples, this consideration overrides all others, because anxiety about possible pregnancy uses up so much time and energy. For others, the pill or abstinence are the only acceptable methods of birth control because pregnancy is intolerable and abortion is not an acceptable option.

The pill can be taken at a time when people are not distracted by sexual responses, a major factor in its dependability. It is comparable in safety to other methods.

Its beneficial side effects include the alleviation of premenstrual tension and of painful and/or heavy menstrual periods. Women taking it have a lower incidence of benign breast tumors and ovarian cysts.

RISKS. Most women can take the pill without serious side effects. The few women for whom the pill would pose serious risks can usually be identified with adequate screening and yearly medical check-ups.

Pills should NOT be taken by women who have ever had internal blood clots, inflammation in the veins, cystic fibrosis, coronary artery disease, cancer of the breast or reproductive organs, or recurrent jaundice of pregnancy.

Nor should pills be taken by women who are pregnant or nursing, over age forty, have high blood pressure, impaired liver function, or undiagnosed vaginal bleeding.

If any of the following conditions exist, a woman should take the pill only after carefully weighing all alternatives with her clinician: varicose veins, heart or kidney disease, endocrine disorders, chloasma, diabetes or pre-diabetic symptoms, very irregular, painless periods, uterine fibroid tumors, asthma, migraines, epilepsy, depression, or smoking more than fifteen cigarettes a day after age thirty.

A woman with none of the above conditions should be screened for possible problems of which she might be unaware. A complete medical history should be taken, including a description of her smoking habits. Her blood pressure and weight should be recorded, her urine tested, and she should have breast and internal pelvic examinations. A Pap smear should be taken. This screening should be repeated at least once a year, and many clinicians are recommending more frequent blood pressure checks.

Further screening is accomplished by the woman as she takes the pill.

90

Those who experience side effects usually find that they disappear within the first few weeks. Symptoms that should be reported to one's doctor or clinic if they persist are: nausea, fluid retention (causing a bloated feeling, sore enlarged breasts, swollen legs, or rapid weight gain), increased appetite, inappropriate depression or irritation, vaginal or vulval itching, less interest in sex, changes in skin and hair, or spotting or bleeding between periods. A change in habits may be suggested: for example, cutting down on sodium (salt, diet pop) may reduce fluid retention; taking the pill after a full meal may reduce nausea; or, a change in the pill prescription may be appropriate.

Medically dangerous side effects from the pill are very rare. A woman should STOP taking the pill and consult her doctor or clinic immediately if any of the following symptoms occur: persistent pain in the arms and legs; numbness or weakness; chest pain; shortness of breath; sudden severe headaches, with or without nausea and vomiting; undiagnosed dizziness or fainting; disturbances of vision or speech; or severe abdominal pain.

The remaining question regarding risks associated with the pill has less precise answers. Are there long-term effects that persist or may appear after a woman has stopped taking the pill? Pills have been used twenty years. Since 1960 evidence about long-term effects is only beginning to accumulate and much of it is confusing, partly because prescribed dosages of the hormones in the pill have steadily and significantly decreased during that time.

British researchers in 1977 published reports suggesting that the pill makes a woman more susceptible to cardiovascular disease and that such effects may persist long after she stops the pill. That is why a woman's smoking habits are imporant if she is considering the pill. Smoking creates considerably more strain on her heart and blood vessels than the pill; together they are more powerful than the sum of the effect of each without the other. For most young women who don't smoke, these effects on the circulatory system appear to be marginal; present research suggests that non-smokers under 35 can take the pill with minimal risk for five years if they are checked at least annually for possible medical contraindications.

While it has often been suggested that the pill might increase susceptibility to cancer, not only has no such effect been demonstrated, but it is

91

more likely that the pill reduces susceptibility to some cancers. Women taking the pill develop fewer benign breast lumps and ovarian cysts than women who don't take it and women with those conditions are more likely to develop cancer than other women.

Women who take the pill are more likely to be susceptible to gall bladder disease than those who don't; if it develops or if a woman has had it, she should not take the pill. Benign liver tumors are rare, but their incidence appears to increase with the use of the pill. The presence of polyvinyl chloride wastes in the water supply apparently combines with the pill to increase the incidence of such tumors, suggesting the difficulty of assessing the effects of the pill without careful study of the other influences on a woman's health.

Evidence suggests that the pill can cause congenital defects in children conceived while a woman is taking the pill or within 90 days of her stopping the pill. For this reason, people are advised to stop the pill and use another contraceptive for at least three months before trying to conceive.

Longitudinal studies in progress since 1968 are indicating that in spite of fears to the contrary, the pill cannot be blamed for infertility after a woman has taken it. Infertility occurs in about 10 percent of women who want to conceive. Some become fertile as soon as they stop the pill. The statistical average for post-pill return to regular ovulation-menstruation patterns is two to three months. For a few, desired conception may be delayed, but delivery occurs within 42 months of discontinuing the pill in all but 11 percent of couples whose fertility had not been proved prior to pill use. A number of factors, of course, can affect a couple's fertility at any given time.

The IUD

HOW IT WORKS. The IUD (intrauterine device) is made of soft plastic, which is sometimes combined with copper or a hormone, and is inserted by a clinician during an office visit. Unless expelled, it is about 98 percent dependable in preventing pregnancy by inhibiting the implantation of a fertilized egg on the uterine wall. It may also initiate a uterine reaction destroying the egg and/or the sperm, and it may speed transport of the fertilized egg through the tube so that it reaches the uterus too early in its development for implantation.

BENEFITS. The IUD does not require rational control at the time of sexual response because it is inserted by a clinician and stays in place in the uterus until a woman has it removed. The user's only responsibility is to check it at least once a week and immediately after a period by inserting her (clean) finger into her vagina to feel the IUD string which protrudes through the cervix. Thus, for women who can wear it without problems, it requires less of the user than any other method and its effectiveness rate is high.

RISKS. Nearly all IUD risks are greater for women who have never been pregnant. Sometimes an IUD cannot be inserted because a woman's uterus is too small or because she has a vaginal infection, or a history of pelvic inflammatory disease (PID), ectopic pregnancy, or an abnormal Pap smear.

Insertion is uncomfortable for some women and, though it is quick, it is occasionally followed by intermittent cramping for as long as several days. Increased cramps and menstrual flow usually accompany IUD use, and women who already have heavy painful periods are less likely to adjust to an IUD. If periods last longer than ten days (including spotting), a woman should consult her doctor about removing the IUD because of the increased incidence of infection with extended menstruation.

The most significant risk is that IUD users have a 3-7 times greater chance than nonusers of developing PID which may recur many times and threatens fertility. The risk of infection is increased if a woman or her partner is sexually intimate with others. Fatal infections have occurred in women who become pregnant with an IUD in place. This means that as soon as an IUD wearer's menstrual period is TWO WEEKS OVERDUE, SHE MUST HAVE A PREGNANCY TEST and, if the test is positive, arrange to have the IUD removed immediately. A woman whose periods are irregular should have a pregnancy test any time her cycle extends to 6-8 weeks even though such long cycles have not previously indicated pregnancy. The risk of ectopic pregnancy (outside the uterus) is higher with an IUD than with any other form of birth control.

Condom and Foam

The consistent, careful use of BOTH condom and foam at the same time results in 99 percent dependable contraception. (See detailed description of each method below.)

The Condom

HOW IT WORKS. The condom is a synthetic rubber or natural membrane sheath which is unrolled over the penis as soon as erection occurs and prevents sperm from reaching an egg.

BENEFITS. Condoms are readily available without prescription at family planning clinics and drugstores. They provide protection against VD. There are no physical side effects unless a person is allergic to latex, in which case he can use one of the more expensive condoms made of natural animal membranes. Their use allows male participation in birth control responsibilities. If used with foam, dependability approaches that of the pill; used alone it is about 80 percent dependable.

Prelubricated condoms reduce friction and irritation experienced by some couples. Condoms prevent the rare allergic reactions of some women to semen and, by inhibiting the spread of VD, they may diminish the likelihood of cervical cancer in some women.

RISKS. Careless use of the condom may account for the fact that condoms used without foam are no more than 80 percent dependable. To reduce the possibility of the condom's breaking or leaking at the open end, a half-inch space without air must be left at the tip to collect semen at ejaculation. Putting the condom on after genital contact has occurred may be too late because sometimes there is a small drop of semen with many sperm which appears before ejaculation and of which a man is unlikely to be aware. Withdrawal of the penis without holding the open end of the condom close to the base of the penis may leave sperm within the vagina. Friction causing tearing of the condom during intercourse can be avoided by using lubricated condoms or by applying spermicide as lubrication. Vaseline® can deteriorate the condom and should never be used as a lubricant.

Some people complain that the condom inhibits sexual spontaneity, a problem that can be diminished if the partner learns to put it on as part of sexual play.

94

Foam/Suppositories

How they work. Spermicides provide a barrier inhibiting passage of sperm into the uterus. They are marketed as creams and jellies (made for use *with* a diaphragm and less effective without one), foams, and suppositories. Foam is packaged in a vial and inserted with an applicator deep into the vagina, creating a spermicidal barrier that lasts about one-half hour after insertion. Suppositories dissolve into spermicidal foam in 15-20 minutes and so protection is not immediate on insertion as with foam, but it lasts up to an hour. Even within those time limits, additional foam or suppositories must be reinserted for each act of intercourse, because vaginal secretions and ejaculation tend to wash away the spermicide.

Benefits. Used with the condom, foam or suppositories are about 99 percent dependable and available without a prescription to anyone at family planning clinics and drugstores. It is useful as a back-up method (for pills, while waiting to start them and during the first 10 days of the first cycle or if one stops taking them; if the IUD is expelled; or with condoms). Foam is rarely associated with side effects and offers some protection against VD (not as much as the condom).

Risks. Suppositories appear to cause burning, itching, and susceptibility to infection in men and women more often than foam. If either partner appears to be allergic to a brand, try another. Used alone, spermicides have a failure rate as high as 30 percent. Sexual spontaneity may be disturbed less if the partner helps with insertion. Many people dislike the taste, so oral-genital play may be more satisfactory before insertion of foam. It is impossible to tell when one is going to run out of most brands of foam, so one should keep an extra vial. Spermicides can be confused with "feminine deodorants," so be sure the product being used is clearly labeled "contraceptive." Contrary to advertising claims, suppositories are NOT more dependable than other spermicides and should be used with condoms.

Less-Dependable Birth Control

Rhythm

How it works. Women usually ovulate only once during a menstrual

95

cycle. If a woman can identify the time of ovulation, abstinence from genital contact at this time should achieve contraception. It is very difficult, however, to be sure when ovulation occurs, let alone to predict it accurately. A woman can ovulate more than once a month; sometimes it is stimulated by arousal or delayed by tension, travel, weather changes, etc. To make matters more complicated, the egg can be fertilized up to 24 hours after it is released from the ovary, and sperm can live 72 hours or more while waiting for the egg in the uterus or tubes.

People interested in rhythm should learn at least three ways of calculating the probable time of ovulation. The first is called the calendar method. When a woman has kept an accurate record of her periods for at least a year, she can use the following chart. For example, if her periods have come every 28-32 days, she will probably avoid conception if she has no genital contact from the 10th through the 21st day of her cycle.

Shortest cycle	First unsafe day	Longest cycle	Last unsafe day
21 days*	3rd	21 days	10th
22 days	4th	22 days	11th
23 days	5th	23 days	12th
24 days	6th	24 days	13th
25 days	7th	25 days	14th
26 days	8th	26 days	15th
27 days	9th	27 days	16th
28 days	10th	28 days	17th
29 days	11th	29 days	18th
30 days	12th	30 days	19th
31 days	13th	31 days	20th
32 days	14th	32 days	21st
etc.	etc.	etc.	etc.

*Day 1 is the first day of menstrual bleeding

Second, if a woman takes her basal body temperature (the lowest temperature in a 24-hour period, usually recorded just before getting up in the morning) daily on a thermometer calibrated for each tenth of a degree, and records it on a graph paterns for six months, she may be able to identify ovulation through patterns of temperature fluctuation. A long-term record is necessary because the influence of ovulation on temperature must be assessed independently of other stress, illness, fatigue, strange food, etc.

The third way to increase the chances of identifying the time of ovulation is to learn to observe changes in one's cervical mucous. Each of these techniques takes time to learn. Professional coaching is highly desirable, though there are several books that give useful information.

BENEFITS. Learning more about how the body works can be exhilarating, especially when the partner cares and participates in the observations, record keeping, and calculating the safe times. No pills need be taken, and the only device to be inserted is the thermometer. Although daily observations are necessary, nothing need be done at the time of sexual arousal. The method is acceptable to the Roman Catholic Church.

RISKS. Failure rates are not predictable; 60-75 percent dependability is probably optimistic for most people, although highly motivated couples who have developed skills of observation and interpretation may achieve a 2-3 percent failure rate. Tolerance of unplanned pregnancy or abortion is essential.

There are many days when a couple must abstain from genital contact; some couples can approach this creatively and be happy with alternative sexual interactions, but for some, abstinence from genital contact creates problems in the relationship. In addition to emotional demands, the method requires accuracy and discipline in daily observations.

Withdrawal

HOW IT WORKS. The man withdraws his penis from the vagina and vulva before ejaculation so that no semen touches the woman's genitalia.

BENEFITS. No special equipment, no medical exams or prescriptions are required. It is available at any time to a man who has mastered the skill.

RISKS. The failure rate is high, especially among couples who are not sexually well-acquainted. The man must be able to control the time of ejaculation. Even if he has that control, a small drop of semen, of which he is unaware, may be deposited in the vagina before ejaculation. Both men and women may find withdrawal sexually frustrating.

97

Non-Methods of Birth Control

Douching and "Feminine Hygiene" Products

Douching does NOT work as a contraceptive. It may, in fact, aid conception by pushing sperm toward the cervix or by washing out spermicide. Unless a particular douche is recommended by a doctor to treat an infection, it should be avoided. The vagina is self-cleansing.

Advertising may give a false impression that some "feminine hygiene" products have a contraceptive effect. Many doctors feel that deodorants and douches increase susceptibility to vaginal infection or irritation. The most effective feminine hygiene is a regular bath or shower.

"Morning-After" Birth Control

Few birth control options are available by the morning after and none is very satisfactory. When people have had intercourse without contraception and hope to avoid pregnancy they have the following choices.

1. DO NOTHING. There is no more than a 30 percent likelihood that one act of intercourse will result in pregnancy. If one can cope with a possible pregnancy or abortion, waiting until the next expected period may be best. A urine pregnancy test is not diagnostic until at least 42 days after the last menstrual period.

2. HAVE A POST-COITAL INTRAUTERINE DEVICE (IUD) INSERTED. This is almost 100 percent dependable and provides a continuing method of fertility control. The IUD must be inserted within 72 hours, the sooner the better, and it is often not possible to do the insertion on short notice. Nor is the IUD suitable for all women. In some cases the uterus is too small or other contraindications are present. A woman with bad cramps and/or heavy menstrual flow may not wish to try an IUD. The particular hazard associated with the IUD is pelvic inflammatory disease (PID), which can be a serious health problem and threaten fertility. IUDs are available at family planning clinics and from some private doctors by emergency appointment.

3. TAKE THE "MORNING-AFTER PILL." This is a large dose of Diethyl Stilbestrol (DES) which is approved by the FDA "for emergency situations such as rape and incest if a manufacturer provides patient

labeling and special information.'' To prevent pregnancy, a woman must start taking DES no later than 72 hours after unprotected intercourse. The sooner she starts taking it the more likely it is to prevent pregnancy. (NOTE: DES offers NO on-going contraceptive protection. A woman who takes it must use another method of birth control for subsequent sexual imtimacy.)

There is concern about changes in children whose mothers have taken DES during pregnancy. These can include cancer in female children and infertility in male offspring. Therefore, DES is not prescribed for women known to be pregnant, nor is it to be used if a possible pregnancy would be continued. Some physicians require a pregnancy test and/or a physical examination before prescribing DES to attempt identification of pre-existing pregnancy or other contraindications.

Recent studies suggest that mothers exposed to DES during pregnancy may have a higher incidence of breast cancer in later life. Although the doses of DES used in the cases studied were much larger than those used as ''morning-after'' contraception, this consideration is particularly pertinent in women with a family history of breast cancer.

Immediate, transient side effects from DES include nausea, headaches, or dizziness, controllable with prescription medication. Taking the morning-after pill may be followed by late menstruation, raising the possibility of pregnancy, and requiring examination.

Sterilization

Sterilization is a surgical method of *permanent* birth control. It has usually been requested only after the desired family size has been achieved or when illness or other problems make it necessary. Recent concern about population has led to extensive publicity about sterilization and it is among the most widely used methods of birth control. There are doctors and clinics who will perform the operation for young people who have had no children. Detailed information can be obtained from the Association for Voluntary Sterilization, Inc., 708 Third Avenue, New York, New York 10017.

Male Sterilization is achieved by a vasectomy, a minor procedure, usually performed in a doctor's office. A small segment is removed from each of the two tubes called vas deferens which carry sperm from the

99

testicles. The cut ends of the tubes are tied off and sperm, which compose a minute fraction of the ejaculate, are produced as always but are absorbed easily by the body. Ejaculation occurs exactly as it does before a vasectomy; sexual activity is in no way altered. Sometimes undesirable psychological reactions occur.

Female Sterilization involves tying off the Fallopian tubes, thus preventing the egg from traveling to the uterus or the sperm from reaching the eggs. It does not change a woman's sexual desire or her monthly periods. The tubal ligation is more complex than a vasectomy, requiring an abdominal incision. Until recently, most American doctors have performed tubal ligations only under general anesthesia, requiring a hospital recovery period of from 3-7 days. Two newer methods, laparoscopy and the even simpler mini-laparotomy, can be performed on an outpatient basis at less expense.

Pregnancy

When a woman has had genital contact with a man, conception and pregnancy can occur. When pregnancy is desired, there is no need to see a doctor until the first pre-natal visit, recommended by most obstetricians at the end of the third month of pregnancy.

On the other hand, the woman who senses with dismay that she might be pregnant and is reviewing all her options (abortion, adoption, single, or married motherhood) may wish to discuss her situation with a trained counselor. If abortion is among her possible choices, she would act quickly to ascertain whether she is pregnant when she has any of the following symptoms: *a missed or reduced menstrual period* is particularly significant if her periods are usually regular; *breast enlargement and/or tenderness* perceived when the menstrual period is 7-10 days or more late; *nausea* often felt particularly in the morning and sometimes accompanied by vomiting; *unusual fatigue;* and/or *increased frequency of urination*.

One or more of these symptoms can be related to pregnancy; all of them may have other causes (including the pill, the flu, anxiety about pregnancy, etc). If in doubt a woman should consult her doctor or clinic.

Pregnancy Testing

A urine test for pregnancy usually gives an accurate result when the menstrual period is about two weeks late or the pregnancy is about one month along. There are more false negative than false positive results. If a pregnancy test is negative and the absence of normal menstrual bleeding persists, a woman considering abortion must repeat the test within one week. A gynecological exam by an experienced clinician can usually confirm pregnancy test results by the time a pregnancy is six weeks along. Family planning clinics usually perform the test by appointment for a fee. Pharmacies sell an at-home pregnancy test for about $10; its disadvantages are: (1) it works only once and to repeat the test costs another $10; and (2) experience in reading pregnancy tests is important for accurate interpretation of the results. Many women, however, have used the test successfully and appreciated being able to perform it on their own.

Some doctors and clinics are able to arrange a blood test for pregnancy that gives 98 percent dependable results as early as 10 days after conception. The test is of limited practical value (see "menstrual extraction," below) except in unusual circumstances and, at the present time, is not available everywhere.

Abortion

Abortion has been legal throughout the United States since the Supreme Court ruled in January, 1973 that no government may interfere in a private medical decision.

Early abortion legally performed by a competent clinician in a sanitary setting is nearly always a benign medical procedure. Physical complications or after-effects from abortion are very rare; medically speaking, early abortion is significantly less risky then carrying a pregnancy to term, and recovery is much faster. A woman should go to her doctor or clinic for a post-abortion check-up 3-4 weeks after the procedure. During the intervening time she can nearly always engage in her usual activities. If she experiences excessive bleeding, cramping, or fever, she should consult her clinician and rest. She must abstain from intercourse, oral-genital contact, douching, or the use of tampons until her check-up because of the possibility of introducing infection into the birth canal

101

before the uterus is healed.

Although physical effects are minimal for most women, confronting unwanted pregnancy is emotionally draining. Resolving conflicts surrounding the choice to have an abortion is a straightforward process for some, but it can be complex for others. It is especially difficult for people who never thought of themselves as needing to consider the choice. Because there is no social consensus about the acceptability of abortion, many women struggling to decide what to do about unwanted pregnancy feel socially isolated and need to discuss their feelings with friends, family, clergy, or other experienced counselors before and after the procedure.

Clear, mutually supportive communication with the partner is a significant factor in a woman's ability to accept her need for an abortion.

Early diagnosis of pregnancy is important for the woman considering abortion and can usually be accomplished (see ''Pregnancy Testing'') about two weeks after the first missed menstrual period or six weeks after the first day of the last normal menstrual period.

Techniques of Abortion

VACUUM ASPIRATION. The most common and the safest means of abortion available at the present time is to dilate the cervix and remove the products of conception from the uterus with suction. Up to 12 weeks after the first day of the last normal menstrual period an aspiration can be performed under local anesthesia. It can be done in a doctor's office, a clinic, or in the hospital without an overnight stay. Recovery is almost immediate, though major activity is unwise for a day or two following the procedure. Vacuum aspiration procedures are performed in some hospitals under general anesthesia (which creates greater medical risk than abortion itself). Where an overnight stay is required, the cost is much higher. In some clinics, suction procedures are performed under general anesthesia without an overnight stay at less cost.

MENSTRUAL EXTRACTION. A vacuum aspiration (usually costing somewhat less than routine abortion) is performed when a menstrual period is 1-10 days late and the urine pregnancy test is negative. Most doctors do not recommend this very early abortion because it results in more incomplete procedures and more excessive bleeding and infection.

102

Furthermore, as many as half of the women requesting the procedure are found to have had no pregnancy when the aspirate is checked microscopically; those women have experienced pointless cervical dilation. If circumstances necessitate an early procedure, it is highly desirable to confirm pregnancy with a blood test (see "Pregnancy Testing").

D AND E (Dilatation and Evacuation). A procedure involving cervical dilation, suction, forceps, and curettage can be done from the 12th to the 16th or 17th week from the first day of the last normal menstrual period. Although it is apparently the safest method for second trimester abortions, the technique presently is available in only a few metropolitan areas. Fees are somewhat higher than those charged for first trimester abortions.

INSTILLATION. These procedures are used from 16-24 weeks and are accomplished by injecting hypertonic saline solution, prostaglandins, and/or urea into the uterus. The injection induces labor and delivery and usually kills the fetus. The abortion is completed in 18-36 hours. A hospital stay is necessary. The procedure is much more demanding (physically and emotionally), than the techniques available earlier in the pregnancy. Medically risks associated with instillation procedures are about equal to those of carrying a pregnancy to term. The cost is $900 and up.

Sexually Transmitted Diseases

Sexual activity can lead to the spread of diseases, which are generally classified as "sexually transmitted diseases" (STD — a broader category than the traditional "VD"). The organisms causing these infections live in the warm moist mucous membranes of the mouth, the genitals, and the anus and rectum; the diseases are passed from one person to another by direct contact of any infected area with any or all of the other areas.

Until the development of vaccinations against VD, the only complete protections against infection are monogamy or abstinence. The condom offers some protection. Unfortunately, the pill and the IUD appear to increase a woman's susceptibility if only because the couple is not using a condom.

That VD is an epidemic in this country today is ironic because for

103

most of the infections there are cures if they are treated in time. There are several causes for failure to treat VD. One is that symptoms may not be apparent in one or both partners or in an early stage of the disease. A more complex cause is our social uneasiness about VD; infected individuals either deny they might have it or are ashamed or afraid to request help and information. It is, however, preferable to know that one does not have an infection.

The infected individual can take the responsibility of notifying people with whom she/he has had sexual contacts or the Health Department VD advisor will do so; sexual partners are the only individuals notified and only after a positive diagnosis. Private doctors and the Family Medicine Centers respond in the same way.

The best time to see a doctor is as soon as a person notices symptoms but, as is apparent in the descriptions below, it is possible to be infected without symptoms, and anyone who suspects contact with an infected individual should seek help. It is imporant to inform the clinician of all kinds of sexual activity regardless of the location of symptoms. For example, anal intercourse and oral-genital contacts spread infections as readily as penile-vaginal intercourse. Even manual-genital contact can spread infectious organisms.

GONORRHEA. Symptoms in men are discharge of pus from the penis and/or a burning sensation on urination appearing 2-10 days after contact with the vagina, anus, or mouth of an infected person. Symptoms are less likely to be apparent in the vagina, anus, or mouth. Recent studies suggest that about two out of three infected men have symptoms. Fewer women notice symptoms, which may include vaginal discharge, abnormal vaginal bleeding, or an unusually painful menstrual period. Because the infection may be asymptomatic, a woman should have a test performed with her annual pelvic exam or request a test as soon as she suspects exposure. Sometimes gonorrhea can be diagnosed by microscopic examination of the discharge; more often, a laboratory culture is necessary, requiring 2-5 days.

Treatment recommended for gonorrhea is an injection of a high dose of penicillin in conjunction with a pill (''Probenecid''), which increases the effectiveness of the penicillin. A person allergic to penicillin must inform the doctor; alternative antibiotics can be used.

If gonorrhea remains untreated it may be spread to others and it may

104

cause, anywhere from 1-50 years later, a number of painful conditions (e.g. arthritis, meningitis). It is one of the causes of PID in the female. It may cause sterility in men and women and it may lead to narrowing of a man's urethra, necessitating repeated dilation by the physician to permit urination.

SYPHILIS. The first symptom of syphilis is a small, painless, open sore appearing 2-4 weeks after sexual contact on the genitals, in the rectum, or the mouth. This sore may not be noticed; anal intercourse (either homo- or hetero-sexual) is one way of spreading syphilis without a noticeable sore. The sore usually heals without treatment in about six weeks. Eight weeks to six months later, new symptoms may appear including highly contagious lesions of the genitals or mouth, swollen glands, rash and/or fever. These symptoms may be mild to moderately severe and disappear. Diagnosis can be made from a blood test, which must be performed at least two weeks after the appearance of the sore (4-6 weeks after contact with the infection). Repeated blood tests may be necessary.

Penicillin or an alternative antibiotic is the preferred treatment. If syphilis is not treated, although the disease is sometimes contagious through the second stage, two-thirds of infected individuals suffer no further symptoms, but the remaining third may experience serious, even fatal disturbances of the brain and other parts of the body. A mother infected with syphilis may give birth to a baby with congenital malformations.

HERPES. Herpes infections are being diagnosed more often than gonorrhea and syphilis. Herpes is a virus that causes cold sores (fever blisters) around the facial lips and similar painful sores on the vulva, vagina, penis, and/or scrotum, which last 8-10 days or longer. These infections are causing considerable concern for a number of reasons: (1) they are appearing among increasing numbers of individuals; (2) to date there are *no cures*; (3) they are likely to recur in the same areas whether or not there is renewed contact; (4) a woman can transmit the infection (as is the case with gonorrhea or syphilis) to her baby as it is born, causing serious illnesses such as encephalitis or meningitis, which can lead to mental retardation or even death; and (5) a possible relationship between Herpes and cervical cancer is under investigation.

In spite of there being no cures it is important that an individual have

105

sores diagnosed; to avoid spreading the disease, a person with a Herpes infection must abstain from sexual contacts while the sores are present. Sometimes a clinician can prescribe symptomatic relief, and the sores should be encouraged to dry. To protect the newborn infant, a Caesarian section is performed when a mother has Herpes sores on her vulva or vagina or cervix; sometimes a Caesarian section is indicated for a woman who has had a genital Herpes infection at any time in the past.

TRICHOMONAS. This parasite infection has similar symptoms to monilia. The discharge is usually more watery and has an unpleasant smell. Although a variety of treatments have been used, the only one that has been effective is "Flagyl," taken by mouth. It has been shown to be carcinogenic in mice when they are given large doses throughout their lives and possibly in rats. The FDA believes the risk of human carcinogenesis is low, but unnecessary use of the drug should be avoided. It is reserved for persons in whom the disease has been confirmed and their sexual partners. The disease is usually sexually transmitted, though a male rarely has symptoms.

CYSTITIS. The bladder infection, common in women and rare in men, was often called "honeymoon cystitis" because frequent sexual activity can facilitate the access of bacteria to the bladder. The symptoms may develop very suddenly: a burning pain on urination and a frequent, urgent desire to urinate though only small amounts of urine may be passed. These infections do not go away by themselves; one should see a doctor as soon as cystitis is suspected in order to simplify treatment and prevent serious complications. The treatment is usually sulfa or a similar drug.

CRABS. Crab lice are usually found at the base of pubic and perianal hairs where they suck blood. They cause itching. They are contracted through close personal contact, usually skin to skin, and also from toilet seats, beds, and clothing. Clothing should be washed in hot water, dry cleaned, or left unused for three or four weeks, during which time the lice will starve to death. They are treated with a prescription lotion, ointment, or shampoo.

VENEREAL WARTS. Genital warts are caused by a virus and may be sexually transmitted. They appear one to three months after contact, on the penis, the scrotum, in the vagina, on the vulva, the cervix, and around or in the anus. Diagnosis can usually be made by appearance, without laboratory tests. Treatment (surface application of podophyllin by a clinician) usually causes the warts to fall off within a few days. In some cases a second treatment is necessary. If genital warts are large, they must be removed surgically.

Other Genital Infections

PID (Pelvic Inflammatory Disease)

PID, inflammation of the uterus, ovaries, and/or tubes, was previously thought to occur only as a result of gonorrhea; it is becoming clear that a number of infectious organisms can cause PID, though there are no readily available laboratory tests to determine which ones. A clinician makes the diagnosis on pelvic examination; symptoms may include an unusually painful menstrual period, heavy menstrual flow, severe abdominal pain, and/or generalized abdominal discomfort. Treatment with antibiotics is usually effective, but, once a woman has had it, she has a 33 percent chance of recurring infection — a matter of continuing concern because even one such infection can damage the tubes and cause sterility. PID occurs more frequently among women wearing IUDs than others, but any sexually active woman, whatever the method of birth control, can have the disease; there are a few cases of PID in women who have never been sexually active. A woman with PID may infect her partner with NGU (below).

NGU (Non-Gonococcal Urethritis)

NGU, also known as NSU (Non-Specific Urethritis), is one of the most common sexually transmitted diseases and is diagnosed in males about four times more often than gonorrhea. It occasionally occurs in men who have only one partner; rarely in men who have never been sexually active. A man who has recently had gonorrhea may be especially susceptible to NGU.

Symptoms of the urethral inflammation are similar to those caused by gonorrhea: pain or discomfort on urination, and/or discharge from the penis. Often the discharge is thin and clear and may be continuous or only noticeable in the morning. In some cases the discharge is thick, white, and creamy like gonococcal discharge. Symptoms appear within a few days to a few weeks after contact. When microscopic examination

107

and/or culture of the discharge determines that the trouble is not caused by the bacteria responsible for gonorrhea, urethritis is "nongonococcal." Tests for the other causes of urethritis (including chlamydia and mycoplasma) are not readily available, but NGU can be treated effectively with tetracycline (or erythromycin for those allergic to tetracycline). *No form of penicillin* is an effective treatment for NGU.

Treatment is important. A man with NGU may infect a sexual partner with PID. Many clinicians believe it is important to treat sexual partners of men with NGU (even if no symptoms are apparent in the partner) in order to prevent reinfection and to avoid potentially serious problems, including urethral strictures in men and infertility or sterility in both men and women. Some men experience a relapse of NGU when under physical or emotional stress.

Vaginitis and Vaginal Discharge

Vaginitis is any vaginal infection or inflammation and may or may not be transmitted sexually. Its symptoms may be pain; pain during intercourse; profuse, irritating or odoriferous vaginal discharge; itching, and/or burning. Women occasionally assume that intercourse is painful only for psychological reasons and keep trying to overcome whatever block is involved by having repeated intercourse. This is counterproductive; repeated painful intercourse may create psychological blocks to future satisfactory sex. Therefore, if intercourse is painful, it is advisable to ask a doctor whether there is evidence of vaginitis. If there is an infection, simple microscopic examination usually reveals the cause. When a woman is told she has "non-specific vaginitis,"there is evidence of infection but it is not clear which organisms are causing the problem. Some of the infections causing vaginitis are sexually transmitted and some are not. Treatment is simple and usually promptly effective. Most women are accustomed to some vaginal discharge. Birth control pills may increase normal discharge, as do infections and irritations. Infections that cause changes (in amount, odor, or color) in the vaginal discharge are monilia, trichomonas, and, in a few cases, gonorrhea. Some vaginas, like some people's skin, can be exposed to all kinds of irritants without adverse reaction. For others, many things may cause problems: douches (especially if it is too often or too strong);

108

"hygiene" sprays; foam; some soaps and bubble baths; and foreign objects (e.g. forgotten tampons or dirty hands).

Monilia

Many women who are not sexually active have "yeast infections"; monilia is rarely transmitted sexually and men rarely have symptoms. Other factors that increase a woman's susceptibility may be birth control pills, pregnancy, diabetes, and antibiotics taken for other infections. Monilia is a fungus and can cause mild to severe vaginal and/or vulval itching, vaginal dryness, painful intercourse, and a thick yellow or white cheezy discharge.

It is easy for a clinician to detect it on microscopic examination. It is cured with an antifungal agent (Nystatin) to be administered locally (in a vaginal suppository or cream) and/or orally. Some women experience recurrent infections and require repeated treatment.

REFERENCES

Cvetkovich, G., and Grote, B. *Psychological Development and the Social Problem of Teenage Illegitimacy.* In Schinke, S., and Gilchrist, L.: Adolescent pregnancy: an interpersonal skill training approach to prevention. *Social Work In Health Care,* 3:159-167, 1977.

Gordon, S. *You Would if You Loved Me.* New York: Bantam Books, 1978.

Ross, S. *The Youth Values Project.* Washington, D.C.: The Population Institute, 1979.

Schinke, S., and Gilchrist, L. Adolescent pregnancy: an interpersonal skill training approach to prevention. *Social Work In Health Care,* 3:159-167, 1977.

Resource Materials

Chiappa, J.A., and Forish, J.J. *The V.D. Book.* New York: Holt, Rinehart and Winston, 1976.

Choices. Denver: Rocky Mountain Planned Parenthood, 1977.

Demarest, R.J., and Sciarra, J.J. *Conception, Birth and Contraception: A Visual Presentation.* New York: McGraw-Hill Book Company, 1976.

Gordon, S. *Facts about Sex for Today's Youth.* Charlottesville, Virginia: Ed-U-Press, 1973.

Gordon, S. *Facts about V.D. for Today's Youth.* Charlottesville, Virginia: Ed-U-Press, 1973.

Gordon, S. *Protect Yourself from Becoming an Unwanted Parent.* Charlottesville, Virginia: Ed-U-Press, 1973.

Gordon, S. *V.D. Claptrap.* Charlottesville, Virginia: Ed-U-Press, 1975.

Gordon, S. *You Would if You Loved Me*. New York: Bantam Books, Inc., 1978.
Guttmacher, Alan. *Pregnancy, Birth and Family Planning*. New York: Viking Press, 1973.
The Handbook Collective. *Birth Control Handbook, V.D. Handbook*. Available for 35¢ each from P.O. Box 1000, Station G. Montreal, Quebec, Canada, HZW ZNI.
Harding, G. *Birth Control*. New York: Pegasus, 1970.
Lieberman, E.J., and Peck, E. *Sex and Birth Control: A Guide for the Young*. New York: Schocken Books, 1975.
Lyman, M. *Sex Facts*. Syracuse, New York: Planned Parenthood of Syracuse, Inc., 1977.
Mazur, R.M. *Commonsense Sex*. Boston: Beacon Press, 1973.
Mier, R., et al. *Elephants and Butterflies – and Contraceptives*. Chapel Hill, North Carolina: ECOS, Inc., 1972.
Turner, U.G. *Herpie: The New V.D. around Town*. Venna, Virginia: Media Fair, Inc., 1977.
V.D. Education in California: A Review of Ideas, Programs, Methods, and Resources. Sacramento, California: California State Department of Education, 1976.
Wilson, R.R. *Contraceptive Education: A Self-Instructional Course*. Chapel Hill, North Carolina: Carolina Population Center, 1974.
Zorabedian, T. *The View from our Side: Sex and Birth Control for Men*. Atlanta: Emory University Family Planning Program, 1975.

APPENDIX

AUDIOVISUAL MATERIALS

AUDIOVISUAL MATERIALS

From: **Perennial Education, Inc.**
1825 Willow Road
P.O. Box 236
Northfield, Illinois 60093

Are You Ready for Sex? 24 minutes, color (Junior and Senior High, Parents)

This film focuses on the difficulties of making decisions about sexual behavior. It encourages open discussion through on-film group discussion of scenarios involving teens making decisions. The film emphasizes values and responsibility in personal decisions.

Would You Kiss A Naked Man? 20 minutes, color (Senior High)

This film presents two adolescents discussing ideas and notions concerning sex and expressions of their sexuality. Both male and female frontal nudity are presented as part of an effort to represent accurately male-female roles, attitudes, and behaviors. It is strongly recommended that the instructor preview this film before showing it.

Hope Is Not a Method. 16 minutes, color (Junior and Senior High, Adults)

A film addressed particularly to the teenager who wants straightforward information about contraception. Covers prescription and drugstore methods and the less effective withdrawal and rhythm methods. Also available in Spanish.

A Family Talks About Sex. 28½ minutes, color (Senior High, Parents)

The purpose of this film is to help parents to communicate with their children — from toddlers to college age — about sex. Topics discussed with children and adolescents include masturbation, privacy, pregnancy, puberty, menstruation, wet dreams, inter-

111

course, the pill, and finally marriage. Delicate situations and questions are handled with sensitivity but also with straight forwardness.

The Trying Time. 20 minutes, color (Parents, Senior High)

In this film, teenagers are shown enjoying one another's companionship, but the soundtrack consists mostly of voices of parents reminiscing about their own youthful traumas and voicing their concerns and feelings about the movement of their children toward adulthood. The film is designed to help viewing parents discuss comfortably the anxiety-laden issues of sex, independent decision making, peer group standards and develop confidence in their ability to communicate with their children on these issues. In the same way, the film may be used with teenagers to lead them to discuss their problems and their parents' attitudes toward them.

Teen Sexuality – What's Right for You? 29 minutes, color (Junior and Senior High)

The intent of this dramatic film is to help teenagers in exploring their own value systems as they relate to sexuality. Boys and girls, independently and in groups, candidly discuss a great variety of observations, including topics of masturbation, pornography, homosexuality, VD and contraception. A teenage couple visits a birth control clinic. Dr. Deryck Calderwood and Dr. Vivian Clark answer teen questions.

Far Cry From Yesterday. 20 minutes, (Junior and Senior High)

This film shows an unmarried teenage couple who accepted an unplanned pregnancy because they "have such a beautiful thing going." Their loving relationship deteriorates quickly, however, as soon as the newborn baby demands constant care, responsibility, planning and, in short, becomes a terrible burden.

Young, Single and Pregnant. 18 minutes, color (Senior High)

A documentary dealing with four young women who reflect on their experiences since becoming pregnant and on their four different solutions: adoption, abortion, marriage, and single parenthood. The film stresses the individuality of every woman's experience and subsequent decision. In documentary style, the camera follows each of the women through characteristic events of her day while she discusses the reasons for her decision and the impact of that decision on her life.

It Couldn't Happen to Me. 28 minutes, color (Junior and Senior High)

One of the major questions asked about young people today is "Why do so many sexually active teenagers not use contraception?" Focusing on the topics of premarital sex, birth control, and pregnancies, the film responds to this question. Discussions are held with young women who have experienced pregnancy, including a group of pregnant teenagers, a girl who gave her child up for adoption, and a girl who had an abortion. Discussion focuses on reasons why these young people did not use birth control during their sexual relations. Included also is another group of students discussing the sexual attitudes of contemporary youth.

When Love Needs Care. 13 minutes, color (Junior and Senior High)

The film portrays in a straightforward manner the actual experiences of a male and a female adolescent being examined and treated for VD. The patients are nervous but honest; the doctors are frank but supportive and reassuring. The film's documentary style places the audience in the position of identifying with the patients and learning, just as they do, of the importance of detecting these diseases early and of contacting sex partners who may also be infected. By removing the fear and mystery surrounding the procedures for diagnosing and treating VD, the film helps the viewer to become better acquainted with the realities of medical attention.

Sex Education: Organizing for Community Action. 23 minutes, color (adult, teacher training)

This film offers basic guidance for those communities considering the development of sex education programs.

Sex Education in the Schools: Philosophy and Implementations. 28 minutes, color (adult, teacher training)

This film presents a basic philosophy of what constitutes an outstanding sex education program.

Birth Control Methods: A Simplified Presentation. (Special Education Programs)

Developed after a 1½ year study of the sexuality of the mentally handicapped. Each kit consists of a captioned filmstrip, filmstrip script, a 25-panel flip chart, and a monograph on *Sexuality and the Mentally Retarded.* Birth control methods and the need for sexual

113

responsibility are presented in simple and repeating illustrations. The diaphragm and rhythm methods are not shown, as they are considered too complex for understanding by the intended audience.

Your Changing Body for Blind Children and Others. (age 10-18)

This guided body exploration is a sensitive approach to the concerns all young people have about their developing sexuality as they mature. The program provides information about puberty with specific instructions to the student to explore through touch his or her body from head to toe. The male/female presentation provides accurate descriptions of body parts and functions and gives a clear image of the other sex. Each kit contains two 40-minute cassettes (one with slang terminology), and a 15-page guide for parents and teachers.

Like Other People. 37 minutes, color (Senior High)

This film deals with the sexual, emotional, and social needs of mentally or physically handicapped individuals. The two main characters have cerebral palsy. Through their actions they communicate a plea for acceptance as "real" people. This love story emphasizes that the emotions shared by disabled persons are like those of all persons in loving relationships. Although the verbal dialogue is sometimes difficult to understand, this adds to the reality of the challenges facing persons with cerebral palsy.

VD and Women. 17 minutes, color (Senior High)

A film to use in teaching the sexually active female about the infections that can be caused by sexual intercourse. Facts and warning symptoms are explained. To alleviate fear of the pelvic examination, a female gynecologist explains every step that is involved and the tools that are used. Discussion of syphilis, gonorrhea, and herpes stress the serious side effects resulting from these infections. Treatment is discussed, and the viewer is taught exactly how to find free VD clinics in her county.

About Puberty and Reproduction. 12 minutes, color (Junior and Senior High, Special Education)

This film is meant to be used with special audiences that need special explanations, either in simple language, sign language, foreign language, or in carefully selected terminology. For this

114

purpose the film is silent and consists of animated, stylized illustrations of the external and internal changes that occur in boys and girls at puberty. A brief outline of pregnancy and childbirth is included at the end of the film.

From: **O.D.N. Productions**
114 Spring Street
New York, New York 10012

Acquaintance Rape Prevention. color (Junior and Senior High)

This is a four film program depicting situations where rape occurs between acquaintances and illustrating the need for assertiveness and better communication skills. Young men and women are constantly striving for attention and affirmation from the opposite sex. Their encounters with each other sometimes deteriorate into games and volatile situations. The films come with well-written discussion guides, role play cards, and student fact sheets.

1. *The Party Game.* (8 minutes)

   Shows how easily ineffective communication can lead to acquaintance rape. She wants affirmation of her attractiveness; he wants casual sex. Their misunderstanding leads to a frightening encounter between the two.

2. *The Date.* (6½ minutes)

   Focuses on sex role stereotypes. Raymond takes Charlotte out on an expensive date, expecting sex in return. He becomes more insistent and Charlotte's fantasy of a perfect evening ends in violent confrontation.

3. *Just One of the Boys.* (8½ minutes)

   Mike is faced with a moral dilemma when his friends insist he participate in sexually attacking Josie, a girl with a bad reputation. Peer pressure and acceptance of labels can trigger acquaintance rape.

4. *End of the Road.* (9½ minutes)

   Assertive behavior can prevent acquaintance rape. Jinny's car breaks down on a lonely night. She accepts help from a man she vaguely knows. She firmly rejects his attempts to exploit the situation and succeeds in averting a potential assault.

115

From: **Cine-Image Productions, Ltd.**
3929 Maquoketa Dr.
Des Moines, Iowa 50311
Too Soon Blues, 25 minutes, color (Junior and Senior High)
A film, portraying a young inner-city adolescent couple's relationship and pregnancy scare. Feelings and attitudes about adolescent sexuality are pointed out in comments from teens throughout the story. Good discussion starter for those dealing with relationships, responsibility, and problem pregnancy.
A Chance of Love. 23 minutes, color (Junior and Senior High)
A companion film to "Too Soon Blues," this film alternates between teen interviews and a narrative story of two inner-city adolescents. On this second film in the series, Jay's and Debby's relationship is carried beyond her false pregnancy into the difficult areas of contraception and adolescent maturity.

From: **Public Health Education Division**
The National Foundation/March of Dimes
Box 2000
White Plains, New York 10602
Woman-Child. about 20 minutes, color (Junior and Senior High)
Presents an overview of the problem of adolescent pregnancy and the risks in terms of health, education, and personal life goals.

From: **Ed-U-Press**
123 Fourth Street, NW
Charlottesville, Virginia 22901
Herpie – The New VD Around Town!
This filmstrip with audio cassette and study guide provides an innovative approach to teach young people about this venereal disease.
Coming to Terms With Our Own Sexuality First.
This is a sixty-minute audiotape of a major talk by Dr. Sol Gordon, well known sex educator.
Breaking the Language Barrier.
Filmstrips or slides. Desensitizes the language of sex as it matches slang terms with their conventional and clinical counterparts.

116

Rollin' With Love.
A film designed to facilitate open discussion of homosexuality.
Kids Who Have Kids Are Kidding Themselves.
This ten-minute filmstrip presents a strong plea for teenage females not to get pregnant. Presents startling statistics and truths about teenage pregnancy which will help youths realistically understand this event.
From: **New Day Films**
P.O. Box 315
Franklin Lakes, New Jersey 07419
Am I Normal? (Junior and Senior High)
This film deals frankly with the concerns, attitudes, and typical experiences of young males in a humorous and warmly human manner. It follows a 13-year-old boy's attempts to gain understanding of the changes he is experiencing as he enters puberty and follows his interactions with his friends, his father, and community health professionals.
From: **Stanfield House**
900 Euclid Avenue
P.O. Box 3208
Santa Monica, California
On Being Sexual
Film and training package for parents of the retarded dealing with the question of when and how to tell about sex.
From: **McGraw Hill**
CRM Films
Delmar, California 92014
Are We Still Going to the Movies? 14 minutes, color (Junior and Senior High)
A trigger film about adolescent sexual conflict. Jack and Dana realize that their relationship is suffering from a lack of communication around sexual issues. The interactions in the film will lead to discussions of role expectations and communications in relationships.
From: **The Institute for Family Research and Education**
760 Ostrom Avenue

Syracuse, New York 13201
Becoming Askable. (Parent Educators)
Video training tape describing the components of a parent sex education training program.
From: **Association-Sterling Films**
P.O. Box 117
Ridgefield, New Jersey 07657
Naturally . . . a girl. 13½ minutes, (Junior and Senior High)
This film explains the biological facts of menstruation and relates menstruation to approaching womanhood. Narration reinforces natural, positive comments by teenagers as they explain candidly what menstruation means to them personally. The questions young girls ask most often are examined and explained.
From: **John Wiley and Sons, Inc.**
605 Third Avenue
New York, New York 10016
Achieving Sexual Maturity, 21 minutes, color
This film deals with the sexual anatomy, physiology, and behavior of both sexes from conception through adulthood. It uses explicit, live photography of nude adult males and females to explain sexual anatomy. It moves, in order, through conception, embryonic development, early childhood, puberty, adolescence, and adulthood; showing parallel male and female development. The film describes ovulation and menstruation in girls and ejaculation in boys. It treats masturbation as a normal sexual activity in both sexes and uses live photography to show masturbation in both sexes. At appropriate times throughout the film, young people express spontaneous feelings and tell individual experiences they've had during the various stages of sexual development.
From: **Children's Home Society of California**
5429 McConnell Avenue
Los Angeles, California 90066
Teenage Father. 30 minutes, color (Senior High)
This documentary-type film presents the often overlooked side of teenage pregnancy: the teenage father. A video camera follows a 17-year-old father-to-be and his 15-year-old girlfriend through the

118

last few months of an unplanned pregnancy. Film sequences include parental reactions, the couple's dilemma over making decisions, counseling sessions with a social worker, and interviews
with the boy's peer group.

Menstruation. 30 minutes, color (Junior and Senior High)
An "unstodgy" humorous film which describes the experience
of a 15-year-old girl and her 16-year-old boyfriend during the week
she gets her first menstrual period. As the film progresses, their attitudes change from embarrassment to more casual acceptance.
Exposes myths and tales surrounding menstruation. Includes an
animated segment explaining the physiological process.

From: **Texture Films**
1600 Broadway
New York, New York 10019

About Sex. 23 minutes, color (Junior and Senior High)
A hip expert in sexuality has a relaxed rap session with a largely
racially mixed group of teenagers in which he openly and honestly
answers a variety of questions. Topics touched on are venereal disease, thoughts and fantasies, body growth, masturbation,
homosexuality, birth control, abortion, and relationships. A frank
film which replaces misinformation with understanding.

Loving Parents. 20 minutes, color (Parents)
The film focuses on sex education in the home with the understanding that parents are the best sex educators of their own children. Several typical situations are presented with group discussion
about methods of dealing with each problem. Parents in the groups
raise concerns about their levels of comfort in discussing sexual
matters and their uncertainty about what is appropriate for their
children. Excellent discussion starter, good for adults and young
adults who are contemplating parenthood.

From: **Guidance Associates, Inc.**
Communications Park, Box 300
White Plains, N.Y. 10602

Young, Single and Pregnant. (2 filmstrips)
This program presents some of the psychological reasons why
young girls become pregnant and discusses how boys feel when

these pregnancies occur. Various options available to pregnant women are discussed, including marriage, abortion, single parenthood, or giving the infant up for adoption.

A representative from Planned Parenthood talks about some of the common, unconscious motivations that lead to pregnancy, including proof of femininity or masculinity, desire to hold onto a boy- or girlfriend and rebellion against parents. Young people discuss why they neglect to use contraception and how they felt when they learned about the pregnancy.

VD: What You Should Know. (3 filmstrips)

The program illustrates how syphilis and gonorrhea enter and attack the body, destroy tissue, damage sex organs, cause sterility, threaten the heart, liver, and other vital organs. It clearly identifies symptoms common to both diseases while stressing that signs of infection cannot always be easily detected in women.

Through a dramatized scenario, students see the confidential nature of the patient-doctor relationship and hear why treatment *must* be performed by a doctor. They also learn about testing and treatment for males and females and how to avoid infection. The program stresses that alerting partners to the possibility of infection is an expression of maturity, fairness, and responsibility.

Venereal Disease: Who Me? (2 filmstrips)

This introduction program is designed to make students aware of the prevalence of VD — specifically, gonorrhea and syphilis — and to teach them about its causes and symptoms. The program clearly explains and illustrates basic facts about the nature of VD germs, transmission, and immediate and long-term effects. True-false quizzes within the program reinforce new knowledge about each disease, and questions are carefully structured to encourage classroom discussion.

Emphasis is placed on the importance of seeking immediate treatment from a private doctor or VD clinic, and instructions are given on how to locate clinics. Students are advised that sound personal standards and sensible behavior are the best protection they can have against VD.

Sexual Values in Society. (2 filmstrips)

As the program begins, young people voice confusion over

conflicting beliefs. A panel of specialists discusses the origin of individual and societal values, emphasizing the importance of developing sound sexual values.

A group of teenagers discuss specific dilemmas faced in daily living. Adult and student panelists suggest guidelines that they found helpful in working out their own value system.

Everything But . . . . (2 filmstrips)

This program goes beyond the physiology of sex to deal with the question of sexual responsibility and the formation of personal values. Young people speak out candidly about love, infatuation, and physical desire and various ways to distinguish these feelings. They probe common, exploitive manifestations of sexuality such as ego gratification at the partner's expense and misuse of the word "love" to achieve sexual conquest. The program goes on to discuss the responsibility for sexual conduct and the consequences of sexual freedom.

Becoming a Woman/Becoming A Man. (2 filmstrips)

The program opens by placing the sexual changes of puberty in the context of general body growth. It stresses that great variations in rates and sequences of development are usual and, in part, inherited by the individual.

The next section deals with specific aspects of sexual development in boys and girls. It is divided into two parts so that the material may be shown either to coeducational classes or single sex groups.

Going Out: How Do You Feel About Dating? (2 filmstrips)

A cross section of young people describe their emotions (such as shyness and anxiety) when dealing with the opposite sex. The program explores sexual options as Dr. Sol Gordon, noted counselor/educator discusses sexual responsibility and other questions: "Is teenage sexuality a moral or developmental question? Can parents successfully control or influence teenage decision making?" The danger of pregnancy and the "double standard" in contemporary life are also considered.

Teacher Training: Family Life and Sex Education. (3 filmstrips)

This in-service training program strives to build teacher proficiency and confidence in conducting successful family life and sex education classes. Recorded sequences from actual classroom discussions provide examples of student-teacher interaction on elementary, intermediate, and high school levels. The program advises teachers to involve students in answering questions whenever possible. This procedure gives students practice in communicating about sex and enables the teacher to gauge the sophistication of the class as a whole.

Parent-Community Orientation: Sex Education in America. (3 filmstrips)

By drawing on the experiences of communities that have developed workable sex education programs, this production enlists parental and community support for such programs. Representatives from four different parts of the country, as well as sex education specialists, discuss class structure, appropriate course content, and teacher training.

This parent-community program stresses that sex education can and *should* be taught within a context that helps young people to understand their sex roles, accept their own sexuality, and establish guidelines and personal standards of sexual responsibility. The importance of teacher training and community support is discussed, and some common causes of controversy are examined.

INDEX

125

126

127

128

Spontaneity in sex, 87
Spontaneous erections, 13
Stage of development, x
Stereotypes, 5, 14, 25
Sterilization, 99-100
    female, 100
    male, 99
Street corner education, 17
Suicide rate, vii
Support from parents and community, 22
Support networks for disabled adolescent, 27
Suppositories (See Foam/suppositories)
Syphilis, 105

T

Talks with parents, 54
Teaching about sexuality, 30
    concrete objects, 33
    models, 32
    movies or film strips, 32-33
    pacing, 30-32
    question-and-answer sessions, 33
    role playing, 32
Teen counseling room, 20
Teen "rap" sessions, 38
Television
    role, 17
    talk show appearances on, 77
Theater groups, 6-7
Thiessen, V., 23
Transformation in sex roles, 14-15
Trichomonas, 106
Tubal ligation, 100

Turf-guarding, 6

U

Unique life-cycle challenges faced by parents,
    53
Unitarian Universalist Association, 67-68
United States Commission on Obscenity and
    Pornography, 54, 62

V

Vaginal discharge, 108-109
Vaginitis, 108-109
Values, 5
    discussions of parents concerning, 57-58
Values clarification, 21, 74
Varenhorst, B., 46
Vasectomy, 99-100
Vending machines for condoms, 86
Venereal warts, 106-107
Vicarious pleasure, 48
Visually impaired persons, 27-28, 30

W

Wet dreams, 13
Withdrawal in parent-child relationship, 57
Withdrawal in sex, 97

Y

Yeast infections, 109
You Would If You Loved Me, 15, 86
Youth Bureaus, 20, 37
Youth hotlines, 37
Youth Values Project, 13-16, 20
Youth unemployment, x, 8